Bristol Radical Pa

150 Years of Struggle

A history of the Bristol Trades Union Council

Bob Whitfield, David Large
and Colin Thomas

ISBN 978-1-911522-69-0

Bristol Radical History Group. 2023.
www.brh.org.uk
brh@brh.org.uk

Brian Underwood, holder of various BTC offices.

"A hundred years ago Bristol offered the rich the good life— fine houses in fashionable Clifton, a life of prosperity. But for working men and women it offered overcrowded slums, back-breaking work and low wages – some got just over a pound for a seven-day eighty-hour week."

"London gas workers were sentenced to one year's imprisonment for daring to strike. Bristol workers formed a council of trade unions to campaign for their release. This was the issue that sparked the creation of the Bristol Trades Council. Today it continues its job."

Brian Underwood Trades Council delegate from the Association of Scientific, Technical and Managerial Staff, May Day 1973.

Creating a parliament of labour

1873–1973

Far too little is known about the history of Bristol's working people. In particular, the history of their trade unions has been much neglected although their existence can be traced back to the eighteenth century. By the time the first *Annual Trades Union Directory* was published in 1861 there were at least twenty-eight trade societies in the city.[1] The Nazis must bear some responsibility for this since many invaluable records perished during the fire raids in 1940–41, including much pertaining to the history of the Trades Council whose centenary year this essay is designed to celebrate. Ironically its first minute book carried the inscription "this book must never be destroyed".[2] Fortunately, Sidney Webb, researching for the famous partnership's *History of Trade Unionism,* made detailed notes in 1901 on the contents of this minute book of the Trades Council from its origin in 1873 until the year of the great London dock strike of 1889 and also preserved at least some of its annual reports, financial statements and rule books. From Webb's notes, together with brief reports in the local press,[3] we learn that the Trades Council owed its existence to a small group of trade unionists led by John Cawsey, who was to serve as its first President,[4] who met at a pub called *The Cock and Bottle* in Castle Green on 26th January 1873 to consider, as they might do today, "the important question of altering the laws affecting trade unionists and in every way to aid any section of the industrial classes in the West of England to organise themselves".[5]

Sidney Webb's notes quite rightly observe that the lack of a permanent body to bring trade unionists from the various individual trade societies in what was hoped would become 'a Labour Parliament for the West of England' had been felt for some years past. Local trade unionists were aware that Bristol was behind most cities of comparable size in lacking a Trades Council[6] and had tried in vain to remedy the

1 *First Annual Trades' Union Directory* (London, 1861) pp4–5.
2 According to the TUC souvenir booklet issued for its meeting in Bristol in 1931.
3 *Bristol Times and Mirror,* 26 January 1873; *Bristol Mercury,* 26 January 1873.
4 He was a tailor and the most prominent trade unionist in the city in the 1860s and 1870s.
5 London School of Economics: Webb Trade Union collection: general history, Section A vol iii ff. 244–281 for the notes.
6 The first Trades Council was formed in Liverpool in 1848 followed by Glasgow (1858), Edinburgh (1859), London (1860), Maidstone (1862), Leeds (1862), Birmingham, Manchester, and Preston (all in 1866), Sheffield (1867), Oldham (1867), Aberdeen (1867), Leicester (1870) and Swansea (1872). See W.H. Fraser, Trades Councils in 1967) p.570.

LONDON TRADES' COUNCIL.

REPEAL OF THE CRIMINAL LAW AMENDMENT ACT.

TO TRADE SOCIETIES,
AND ALL ORGANIZED BODIES OF WORKMEN.

LONDON
TRADES' DEMONSTRATION
Whit-Monday, June 2nd, 1873.

The imprisonment of London gas workers in 1873 sparked the creation of Trades Councils in London and Bristol.

defect. A council of Amalgamated Trades had been launched in 1868 with John Cawsey as its President but it was absorbed the following year by the Board of Trades Delegates, a body chiefly dedicated to organising working-class support for the Liberal Party but this, too, petered out in 1871.[7] The stimulus to try again was provided by a national *cause célèbre,* the savage sentence of one year's imprisonment imposed on several London gas stokers for allegedly conspiring to promote a strike against victimisation. Trade unionists considered Mr. Justice Brett's decision as "contrary to justice, dictated in a spirit of revenge, and if further carried into practice totally subversive of the freedom and speech and liberty of action of all Trade Unionists", to quote one example of the nationwide protest that ensued.[8] John Cawsey and his colleagues had met to launch the Trades Council immediately after holding a public meeting at the Broadmead Rooms to add Bristol's voice to this protest.

In its early years the Trades Council was not a powerful body and in the early eighteen eighties there was more than a possibility that it would go the way of its predecessors. The number of societies affiliated to it during the first year was a bare 15 and by 1890 this had only risen to 24. The membership of these affiliated societies was returned as 2,755 in 1874 and 3,522 in 1878. It had declined to 2,160 by 1885 but recovered

7 BJ Atkinson, *The Bristol Labour Movement, 1868–1906* (unpublished DPhil thesis, Oxford 1969) pp188–190 for these predecessors.
8 I MacDougall, ed. *The minutes of the Edinburgh Trades Council* (Scottish History Society, 1968) p348.

to 3,709 in 1890. Funds were slender in the extreme: at the end of the first year, receipts were £8.5s; on the eve of affiliation to the TUC in 1878 income was £11; and even by 1890 it had only risen to about £27.[9] So hard up was the Council that its delegate to the TUC was expelled in 1881 because his expenses had been paid by a source other than the body he claimed to represent.

The weakness paralleled the experience of Trades Councils throughout the country in these years, although Bristol was an extreme case. The downturn in the trade cycle of the late seventies and early eighties reduced business activity and hit trade unions hard: membership affiliated to the TUC fell from just under a million in 1874 to only 379,000 in 1884. Trades Councils also necessarily suffered from declining support.[10] But, in addition, it has to be recognised that trade unionism in Bristol was weak, especially when compared with the northern industrial areas. It has been estimated that nearly half the entire union membership of the United Kingdom in 1889 was to be found in the six counties north of the Humber and Mersey[11] and it was in the heavy industries, which Bristol lacked, that high percentages of workers were to be found in unions. It was by contrast a city with a multitude of trades with many small craft unions which had grown up, as a writer in *The Beehive* explained in 1868, to protect the skilled worker from "the grasping conduct of many employers" and "from the drunken, careless, improvident disposition of a portion of working men…who were often induced to accept any terms that grasping employers offer and are made the instrument for reducing the wages of the sober, industrious and reflecting".[12] The societies represented in the first year with their membership figures provide the flavour: they include the Rope and Twine Makers (60), Saddles and Harness makers (52), Amalgamated Tailors (100), Amalgamated Coachbuilders (69), No. 1 Lodge Carpenters and Joiners General Union (150), No. 2 Lodge of the same (204), Operative Builders' Labourers (400), Shipwrights (340), Operative Corn Porters (170) and Amalgamated Plumbers (16).[13] The list indicates that modern industry had not entirely passed Bristol by, nevertheless, there were only limited signs of organisation among the dockers, boot and shoe workers and miners of the city and among relatively new groups

9 Balance sheet, 1874: *Western Daily Press 14 May 1877: 18th Annual Report, 1890–1.*
10 HA Clegg, Alan Fox, AF Thompson, *A history of British Trade Unionism since 1889,* vol i, 3.
11 Ibid. i 2
12 *The Beehive,* 6 June 1868.
13 *First Annual Report* (Howell Collection, Bishopsgate Institute).

such as the gasworkers and railway men. No wonder a delegate from Newcastle-on-Tyne, addressing a poorly attended recruiting meeting at the Colston Hall in 1878, when the Trades Council was host to the TUC, commented that in the union movement "Bristol did not occupy the position which it should amongst the large cities".[14]

The Trades Council in Bristol was essentially the creation of the older craft unions, particularly in the building trade. It was long to remain dominated by their leaders and was unable to build up numerically impressive support until Bristol unionism itself underwent major change. Signs of such change can be detected in the late sixties and early seventies[15] but it was not really until 1889 that new unionism made its impact in Bristol and transformed the basis of support, although not the leadership of the Council. It would, however, be misleading to imagine that because it was weak in numbers and resources the Council was unable to command respect or achieve anything before 1889. There is evidence to the contrary both in the political and industrial fields.

Politically speaking, its aims were threefold: to keep Bristol trade unionists in touch with national political developments affecting the working man. This it did chiefly by communicating with the TUC's parliamentary committee which kept a close eye on labour issues in the legislature. Secondly, it sought to establish itself as the authoritative body on which the local establishment turned for information and opinion on matters affecting working men. By the mid-eighties some success had been achieved: for instance, when in 1884 the Bishop [of Gloucester and Bristol] established a prestigious committee to make a substantial investigation of Bristol's poor, the Council was invited to nominate a member[16] and, again in 1885, when the editor of *The Bristol Mercury* wanted a feature on distress in the city, a reporter was sent to interview the President of the Trades Council. Putting the case for the poor, the unemployed and the employee to the public early became and has always remained an important and valuable function of the Council. Thirdly, it sought to bring pressure to bear on the city's MPs and on

14 *Bristol Mercury*. 14 September 1978.
15 E.g., the founding of The Bristol, West of England and South Wales Trade and Provident Society showed that a craft society could and did develop an interest in spreading unionism among labourers.
16 See *Report of the Committee to inquire into the condition of the Bristol poor, presented 22 December 1884, to the Bishop of the diocese.* John Fox, plasterer, general secretary of the Trade and Provident Society for 34 years and for a time President of the Trades Council served alongside two Wills, one Fry, nine Reverends and a Monsignor.

local bodies, such as the City Council, the School Board and Poor Law Guardians, to give favourable consideration to labour questions.

Tactically the Council, reflecting the then widespread belief that politics and unionism should not be mixed, began by being strictly neutral between the existing Liberal and Conservative parties, not even giving official support when its President stood and narrowly lost election to the School Board in 1874. Even this posture produced some effect. For instance at the general election of 1874 when it asked all candidates where they stood on three questions vital to all trade unions—equality in contract between Master and Servant,[17] exclusion of industrial action from the law of conspiracy and the legality of peaceful picketing—the Liberals showed a marked anxiety to stand well with the Council by adopting a more favourable line on these issues than they had originally intended.[18] By 1878, however, the Council, with but one dissentient, had come to believe that more was to be achieved by declaring public approval of the Liberals in the hope that they would reward support by concessions on labour questions and be prepared to endorse working men standing at elections for local bodies.[19] Nevertheless, by 1885 the Council had become dissatisfied with the meagre results of this policy. It was well aware that for some time there had been a growing agitation in the city for direct representation of labour on local bodies and eventually in parliament.[20] Consequently it issued a stirring invitation to "fellow workmen" to subscribe one shilling a year to create a great "Local Labour League" to achieve this. The Council urged that the distinguished part played by the TUC Parliamentary Committee in shaping legislation had demonstrated "the Royal Right of British Workmen to seats in the British Senate" and now when "the long neglected Tillers of the Soil were about to exercise the vote for the first time, 'the toilers of the town' should fraternize with them and 'be astir' to take hold of what was within reach, seats on local bodies even if running a candidate for parliament was still out of their reach".[21] The Council's call was heeded. The Labour League was established and in

17 Bristol trade societies had long been concerned over this issue, see eg. their protests over the Master and Servant bill of 1884 (*Northern Star* 13 April 1844).
18 *Webb notes*, 29, 30, 31 January, 5 February 1874.
19 *Ibid.* 29, 30, 31 January, 5 February 1874.
20 The undercurrent of independent working-class political action in nineteenth-century Bristol is illustrated in Dr J Cannon's pamphlet, *The Chartists in Bristol*, while Dr Atkinson (*op. cit.*) has traced the new phase that began in 1870.
21 City Library for the Address. Bristol stood out along with the Councils in London, Birmingham, Glasgow and Edinburgh in going so far as forming an organisation to achieve labour representation at this time (WH Fraser, *op cit.* p. 417).

1886 scored its first success when John Fox, a prominent member of the Trades Council, was returned unopposed in the School Board elections to the chagrin of the Liberals who had done all they could to take him under their wing and prevent him standing as a Labour [League] candidate. A year later a more spectacular victory was won when R.G. Tovey, who doubled the roles of secretary to the Trades Council and the Labour League, became the first labour councillor by winning St Paul's. In short, the Council can lay claim to having played a substantial if not exclusive role in originating the present-day Labour group on the city council.[22] However, its efforts in 1886 to contest a parliamentary seat were defeated by lack of funds and the still firm commitment of the majority of working men to the Liberal cause.

Nevertheless, throughout its history the main concern of the Trades Council has been with industrial affairs. In the early years it saw its chief function as mobilizing help for member trades in dispute. It tried but substantially failed to create a fund to provide those on strike with the full amount of wages they had been receiving by a levy from all affiliated societies who were to form themselves into a federation officered by the Council. The attempt was imaginative but over-ambitious, for the business depression already referred to meant that the Council and its member societies were forced to be cautious and defensive. More often than not disputes with employers ended in defeat,[23] employers often refused to negotiate or submit to arbitration and frequently resorted to lock outs. Unemployment in the city seems to have been considerable, particularly in the winters of the mid-eighties.[24] However, towards the end of that decade the climate was changing. Even before the great labour revolt in the autumn of 1889 there were signs of militancy and union growth among hitherto unorganised workers. The local seamen who had no union in the 1880s established one in February 1889 with the aid of the President of the Trades Council. The Bristol gasworkers began to form a union in 1888 and by July 1889 were considering amalgamation with the London-based Gasworkers and General Labourers Union led by Will Thorne. In the spring and early summer of 1889, the miners

22 The Bristol Socialist Society, founded in 1884, also played a significant part. The most prominent of the tiny band of Socialist delegates to the Council was John Gregory, the poet-shoemaker at Clifton College, who was Vice-President in 1885.
23 E.g., in 1879 the building trades were compelled to accept a cut in wages which was not restored until 1890.
24 Bristol's first Medical Officer of Health, Dr David Davies, remarked in 1884: "there are so many people out of work or only partially employed in Bristol that the suffering of these classes is intense–greater than I have ever known it." (*Homes of the Bristol Poor by the Special Commissioner of The Bristol Mercury (1884)*, p. 98.)

of Bristol formed the Bristol Miners Association and, led by William Whitfield, its energetic Northumbrian agent, launched a series of strikes or negotiations for a 10% pay rise.[25] Nevertheless, it was clearly the example of the great London Dock strike in the autumn of 1889 which touched off the full scale labour revolt in Bristol.

The Trades Council vigorously collected funds for the London dockers[26] and along with the Gasworkers Union and the Bristol Socialist Society arranged the demonstration to mark their victory at which H.H. Gore, the Christian Socialist, made the most dramatic speech calling on Bristolians to support the Londoners since "they were fighting the battle the same as Bristol men would be fighting".[27] How right he was. Throughout the autumn of 1889 there was an unprecedented uprising often of hitherto unorganised workers, including many women. Strike followed strike in the city, first among the galvanised-iron workers at Lysaght's, then by the gasworkers,[28] the dock workers,[29] the boot and shoe operatives[30] and a host of smaller groups such as the women employed at Bristol's only cotton mill,[31] the tramwaymen, the tobacco workers and so on. Some spectacular victories were won, particularly by the gasworkers and dockers whose 'new unions' gathered thousands of members from a variety of occupations and formed links with their national leaders. Immediately after the Bristol dockers had won their tanner—after a three-day strike compared with the five weeks struggle in London—down came Tom Mann and Bristol-born Ben Tillett, President and Secretary of the new Dockers' Union to hold a mass meeting of many thousands to gather support for an organisation that was eventually destined to become the dominant union in the city and the progenitor of Britain's largest union, the TGWU.

---

25 c.f. the growth of the Boot and Shoe Operatives to a membership of over 600 by 1889. From 1885 they had been sending delegates to the Council.
26 The Londoners reciprocated by sending £60 to aid the Bristolians (H Llewellyn Smith and V Nash, *The Story of the Dockers' Strike* (1889), p.186.
27 *Western Daily Press*, 2 September 1889.
28 *Western Daily Press*, 3–11 October 1889 for this brilliantly effective strike by workers who had not had a pay rise for 15 years: W Thorne, My Life's Battles, pp88–89, and for the general position of gas workers. EJ Hobsbawm, Labouring Men, pp.158–178.
29 *Western Daily Press*, October—November 1889 for their strike.
30 2,000 rivetters and finishers came out on unofficial strike for a 10 per cent increase. (A Fox, *A history of the National Union of Boot and Shoe Operatives*, (1958), p. 163). The cotton mill women also asked for a 10 per cent increase but without success (J Latimer, *Annals of Bristol in the nineteenth century, 1887–1900*, p.14).
31 They also asked for a 10 per cent increase but without success (J. Latimer, *Annals of Bristol in the nineteenth century, 1887–1900*, p14).

Jessie Stephen, BTC's first woman President.

Jessie Stephen was a Trades Council delegate. In her narration for the film, _100 Years of Struggle_, she recounted the labour revolt, in the Autumn of 1892, from the perspective of the women workers involved:

"In its early days, the Bristol Trades Council was not prepared to admit women workers. Those at Redcliffe Confectionery Works were compelled to do overtime on top of a 50-hour week for a wage of 6 and 8 pence 3 farthings. When Sanders, their employer, sacked some of the women workers who had joined the union, their fellow workers came out on strike to support them. The strikers discovered that their employer attended Highbury Chapel, so one Sunday they marched up through Clifton to the church. By now the girls had been out on strike for six weeks and were fed up with Sanders's hypocrisy."

...There they stood. sister-women, if the 'Our Father' were true—ill clad, wet through with the driving rain, hungry...

"Next Sunday the girls marched again. This time they were carrying banners and had the support of the striking dockers and the Bristol Trades Council.

But when they arrived, they found the doors closed against them and they were unable to enter. Three organisers were sent to Horfield prison and the girls failed to get recognition for their union."

*The words of Katharine St John Conway, a member of the congregation and an eye-witness, who, as a result, joined the campaign against Sanders. (from Samson Bryher, *An Account of the Labour and Socialist Movement in Bristol* published by Bristol Labour Weekly).

**Highbury Chapel (now Cotham Parish Church)
by Samuel Loxton.**

The Trades Council certainly played a very active part in the labour revolt of 1889. Individual members of the Council can be found busily counselling strikers and serving on the Strike Organising Committee which emerged to coordinate action all over the city. The Council helped collect the vitally necessary funds to sustain those on strike and took the lead in organising victory demonstrations or protest marches. Nevertheless, it is fairly clear that it was the socialists, and in particular H.H. Gore, who captured the limelight and the enthusiasm of the strikers and it was new officials such as Vicary of the Gasworkers and Gorman of the Dockers, aided by national organisers such as Tom McCarthy,[32] who put in much of the hard work of organising the new unions.

What, then, were the consequences of the upheaval of 1889 for the Trades Council? First, membership increased as never before until by 1898, when Bristol was again host to the TUC, it can truly be said to represent almost the whole trade union movement in the city. In 1890 only 24 societies or branches were affiliated: by 1898 there were 63[33] and thenceforward down to 1914 affiliations hovered around this figure, which meant that probably less than a dozen organisations were not members of the Council. It was rare to find more than one union of consequence that was not affiliated at any particular time.[34] Although some of the new bodies, the miners in particular, were slow to affiliate,[35] division between the older and newer unions, which in Sheffield, for instance, led to the emergence of two rival Trades Councils in the same city,[36] was avoided in Bristol. Almost overnight in the early nineties there was a trebling of the individual membership for whom affiliation fees were paid, from the 3,709 of 1890 to the 8–10,000 which was the usual figure down to 1914. About half of these were members of unions that had emerged in the late eighties.

Nevertheless, the influence of the new unions must not be exaggerated. After their inauguration they long found the going very hard and their true achievement was to survive rather than grow. The employers, temporarily caught off balance in 1889, counter-attacked vigorously and there were inherent difficulties about organising

32 McCarthy was a Limehouse Irishman who resigned in 1889 as secretary of the exclusive Stevedore's Union to become organiser of Ben Tillet's newly formed Dockers Union (J Lovell, *Stevedores and Dockers* (1964) pp. 98, 240). The Liberal press in Bristol habitually regarded him as a sinister troublemaker.
33 *Financial Statement,* 1898.
34 The seamen were only intermittently affiliated.
35 The miners joined in 1897 but the Gasworkers Union did so in 1889 and the Dockers in 1890.
36 See S Pollard et al. *Sheffield Trades and Labour Council 1858–1958.*

effectively among the semi-skilled and un-skilled in a wide range of jobs, as both the Gasworkers and Dockers Unions tried to do. Workers of this kind could be and were so easily replaced by blackleg 'free labour'. No doubt such conditions help to explain why new unions found it expedient to cooperate in the Council with older craft unions for whom the 1890s, especially for those in the building industry, were a boom period in contrast to the previous decade. Indeed, the majority of the newcomers to the Council in the nineties were craft unions, often new branches of existing unions in the building trade which was then probably Bristol's second largest industry in terms of the workers it employed. The Council contained a majority, but happily not an overwhelming one, of delegates from such bodies,[37] and its officers tended to be drawn, though not exclusively, from such circles. John Curle, for example, of the Carpenters and Joiners, became secretary in 1890 and held this key post for many years.[38]

The increased size of the Council meant that when its delegates gathered in force something like a parliament of labour *did* result: by 1907, for instance, 165 delegates were entitled to attend. Consequently, it had become necessary to develop a committee structure to handle business between Council meetings and to pay its secretary a very modest salary. For example, by the Edwardian days of the early 1900s, signs of the development of 'white collar' unionism were apparent from the affiliation of small societies of Life Assurance Agents, Prudential Assurance Agents and the Railways Clerks' Association. The burgeoning educational world, too, was first represented by a society of Council School Caretakers.

What did the Council strive to achieve and what measure of success did it have in the two decades preceding the first world war?

Politically speaking, in the two decades before 1914, the Council continued to campaign for labour representation, but it met with chequered and limited success. As late as 1914, Liberals and Tories still monopolised Bristol's parliamentary representation, and only 7 Labour councillors and one alderman sat on the 92 strong City Council. Nevertheless, the trend was clear: there was growing support in the city

37 In 1907, for instance, of 165 delegates, 39 came from the building trades, 33 from the dockers, gasworkers, miners and builders' labourers; 10 each from the engineers, the printing trades and the boot and shoe workers: 9 from the railway men and the rest from a rich variety of occupations mostly of a craft nature (*34*th *Annual Report*, 1906–7).
38 W Gorman, for long secretary of the Dockers' Union, also served the Trades Council as its treasurer for many years beginning in 1895. John Curle became a Labour councillor for St Paul's, 1896–1904, alderman 1904–1910 and Lord Mayor 1927–8.

Poster advertising the 'Black Friday' march on 23rd December 1892.

for labour representation independent of existing parties and having a distinctive ideology. For an increasing number of workers, such as the young Ernest Bevin, this meant socialism.[39] The Council made a substantial contribution to this development although, as time passed, bodies such as the Bristol Socialist Society, the Independent Labour Party (ILP), the Fabians and, from 1906 onwards, the Labour Representation Committee (on which the Council was powerfully represented) tended to take over more political activity which the Council had pioneered with its Labour League of 1885 and its successor of 1891–1906, the Bristol and District Labour Electoral Association (LEA). This association was basically the political arm of the Council which supplied half of its executive and the offices of President and Secretary. It is worth noting the Council anticipated the solution to the problem of financing the election and maintenance of *bona fide* working men that was to be adopted by the labour movement on the national level years later. For fifteen years the L.E.A. fought for labour representation, slowly adding to Labour's modest strength on the city council, usually but not invariably working in harmony with the political bodies just mentioned whose influence within the Council certainly increased as time passed. On the eve of the first world war the newly elected President of the Council was no longer speaking the mild language of the Lib-Labs but was proclaiming that the "fight between Capital and Labour was becoming more determined and bitter" and that Labour would have to adopt, "far more drastic … and unconstitutional methods if it was to end the cursed system of wage slavery".[40]

Such language no doubt also reflected the Council's experience of industrial conflict in Bristol which was indeed acute both in the early nineties and between 1910 and 1914 when dockers and transport workers launched a series of struggles to better their condition. The most striking incident in the earlier period was the Council's part in resisting the employer's offensive which led to a clash with the city magistrates on 'Black Friday', 23rd December 1892, when cavalry and police charged to clear the streets and a considerable number of casualties wound up in the Infirmary. For months before this the Council had been supporting the weekly demonstrations of the timber workers in the port, who had been locked out by their employers, as well as the strike committee who were seeking union recognition for the women at Sander's Confectionery

39 A Bullock, *Life and Times of Ernest Bevin,* vol i, pp.12–15 for his conversion to socialism.
40 *Western Daily Press*, 6 February 1914.

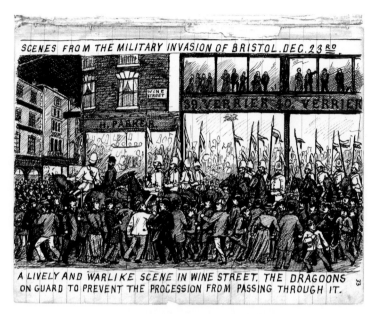

SCENES FROM THE MILITARY INVASION OF BRISTOL. DEC. 23 RD

A LIVELY AND WARLIKE SCENE IN WINE STREET. THE DRAGOONS ON GUARD TO PREVENT THE PROCESSION FROM PASSING THROUGH IT.

The Christmas bells are ringing
The sky is clear and bright
Your masters pray for peace
But are compelling you to fight.
Away with politics—Labour to the front!*

Along the road the soldiers rode
Dispensing sabre cuts
The bobbies drew their truncheons
And bashed in people's nuts
And when perchance they happened to meet
A fellow all alone
They knocked him down
They ran him in
To save him walking home.

*Quotes from Samson Bryher in An Account of the Labour and Socialist Movement in Bristol published by Bristol Labour Weekly, p38 and p45.

factory.[41] Finally, it was planned to hold a mass march from the Grove to the Horsefair. Torches and Chinese lanterns were to be carried since the marchers were to assemble after work at 7pm. City centre shopkeepers became alarmed lest Christmas shoppers be scared away: the police were appealed to and the Chief Constable ruled that no torches or lanterns were to be carried and defined a route avoiding the city centre. The organisers of the march accepted the ruling on lanterns (a fire risk was involved) but denied the right of the police to dictate a route, whereupon the magistrates sought the help of 200 Hussars and Dragoon Guards who were duly sent from Aldershot by special train. The move clearly inflamed a tense situation. The Trades Council furiously condemned "the criminal stupidity" of the magistrates, blamed them exclusively for the ensuing riot and argued that it would never have happened if the magistrates had not been "a non-elective body and chosen exclusively from the employing and capitalist classes".[42] Black Friday long remained a bitter memory in Trades Council circles and was celebrated in defiant songs.[43] More immediately, Black Friday forced the Liberals temporarily on to the defensive since it was a Liberal mayor who called in the troops.

The upshot was a small but significant advance in labour representation. John Curle, the Council's secretary, became Labour's first city magistrate; Frank Sheppard, another Council member, began his outstanding career on the city council by being returned unopposed for St Paul's in 1893; John Sharland, a fellow socialist and Council member had an easy win in St Philip's North; and William Gorman, soon to be the Council's treasurer, won a seat on the Bedminster Poor Law Guardians.

The later nineties were relatively peaceful and at such times the Council were concerned with less dramatic matters such as pressing the City Council to observe the resolution it had adopted, on the suggestion of the socialist H.H. Gore, that contracts for work done on its behalf should contain clauses requiring payment of union rates of pay. Nationally and locally, achieving this was one of the most important if unspectacular victories of Trades Councils. Time and again, in a city

---

41 The Council's sympathy with women workers is noteworthy: earlier it had paid them scant attention, e.g., in 1874 it rejected an appeal for help in organising a union among the girls at the cotton mill and it excluded women from the Labour League of 1885.

42 *Western Daily Press*, 23 & 24 December 1892. The paper defended the authorities but admitted that no inflammatory speeches had been made by the demonstrators; *20*th *Annual Report* 1892–3.

43 One ran: *Not long ago some people said, / We'll march in grand array / Through Bristol's city one fine night /*
With bands and banners gay / Some Chinese lanterns, too / We'll tie on our walking sticks...

FRIDAY'S
POLICE RIOT.

All PERSONS who were INJURED by the Brutality of the POLICE & SOLDIERY on Friday night, are requested to IMMEDIATELY send their NAMES and ADDRESSES, together with an account of such injury, and shortly the circumstances connected with it, to

Mr. W. J. PETHERICK,

The Secretary, Bristol Strike Committee,
British Workman, St. Jude's, Bristol.

Handbill issued after the 'Black Friday' march.

with at least its fair share of employers hostile to unions, the Council tried with varying success to help groups of workers such as the tramwaymen when they were locked out in 1901 or the blind workers in 1910, who were being paid at exploitation rates. It was also particularly concerned in Edwardian days with the plight of the unemployed and with the struggles of the dockers and transport workers. 1908–9 were the worst years for unemployment since the mid-eighties: members of the Council assisted the Right-to-Work Committee (whose secretary was the energetic young carter, Ernest Bevin) in stirring the public conscience and putting pressure on the City Council to institute public works to provide jobs.[44] Council members were also very active in supporting the Bristol dockers in 1910 in their sharp and victorious tussle with local employers and the Shipping Federation whom many rank and file dockers believed were engaging in unscrupulous strike-breaking tactics.[45] Thereafter, however, the Council, for reasons not altogether clear,[46] appears to have played a much more limited role in the very violent upheavals of the summer of 1911 when there seems to have been something of a revolt from below by many rank and file dockers, carters and railwaymen during which troops from Horfield barracks were in action, firing blanks over the heads of excited crowds, and the police made baton charges against strikers who were attacking blacklegs. Indeed, it would appear that there was a substantial breakaway from union leadership at this time and that as a result the Council was unable to co-ordinate the actions of the strikers.[47] Subsequently, in the continued struggles of 1912–13, it was much more effective in such a role.

It would be wrong however to leave the impression that the Council was solely exercised by industrial and political questions: there was another side to the story. It was much concerned to brighten and enlighten the lives of working folk. To the first end it promoted entertainment and social activities: by Edwardian days it was organising outings, tug-of-war competitions and its own brass band, joining with the Co-op to promote concerts, holding an annual garden party (at the Zoo) and, along with the Socialists, winning for Bristol the reputation in the labour movement of being a city where singing and poetry were held in high esteem. Also, from its earliest days the Council was very much concerned with education: as early as 1874 it had invited Dr Percival, the head-master of Clifton College, to address it on technical education, and later many of its members took part in and encouraged evening classes throughout the city. Through its members on the School Board and, later, on the Education Committee, it kept up a consistent pressure for the improvement of educational facilities for the working classes. The Council was also deeply concerned about housing and health. For instance, in 1910 it considered the scourge of tuberculosis in Bristol. One delegate, Ernest Bevin, stood up to argue that bad housing,

44 Among the results was the creation of the lake in Eastville Park.
45 *Western Daily Press*, 21 July 1910.
46 It is difficult to find any evidence of the Council's activity between December 1910 and September 1911.
47 *Western Daily Press*, June-August 1911.

poor food, and factory conditions fostered the disease and that the City Council's health committee was ignoring the problem. He wanted the treatment of the sick to be a charge on the rates and the Council adopted a resolution urging all unions to demand that the City Council should embark on a programme of building houses for the working classes.[48]

Paradoxically, while the first World War witnessed a massive upsurge in union membership in Bristol, the Council suffered some erosion of its effectiveness and curtailment of its role. The major reason for this was the spectacular growth of the Dockers' Union which by drawing into its ranks a great variety of workers made much of the running in the labour movement and to some extent overshadowed the Council.[49] Signs of such development were evident on the eve of hostilities. It was Ernest Bevin, leading local figure among the Dockers' rather than the Trades Council, who called a mass meeting on the Grove to consider the unfolding European conflict and persuaded it to pass a resolution urging British neutrality and calling on the TUC and Labour Party to convene a national conference at once to consider how to prevent the country going to war. Bevin personally declared in favour of a general strike.[50]

Once war began, however, the Council was by no means inactive. It sought particularly to protect workers from its adverse effects. Within a few days of the beginning of hostilities it sent a deputation to the mayor pressing for a citizens' committee to be established to regulate food prices and relieve the unemployment already felt as a direct result of the conflict. The Council probably expressed the outlook of most Bristol trade unionists when its spokesman commented that "whatever their views might be about the war, their only business now was to look after the people and avoid all unnecessary suffering." Its demand, often to be repeated, was that the sacrifices demanded by war should be borne equally by all classes but that given the existing inequalities of society it was inevitable that working folk would bear the brunt unless there was massive government intervention to control the allocation and price of basic necessities.[51] In the early months of the war such a demand united the labour movement in Bristol: even the city's two ILP branches, which consistently opposed the war as a conflict between capitalists

48 *Western Daily Press*, 16 December 1910.
49 Membership figures for the Dockers' Union are not available, but the expansion of its annual income from Bristol from £3,723 in 1914 to £27, 791 in 1919 plainly indicates its substantial growth.
50 *Western Daily Press*, 3 August 1914.
51 *Western Daily Press*, 9 August 1914.

**Bristol Tramways Strike. Scene outside Brislington Depot
during dispute, by E. Coffin, 1901.**

Walter Ayles, BTC member imprisoned for resistance to First World War conscription, and his wife Bertha, also a labour activist.

in which no true socialist could take part, nevertheless supported the Council's demand.[52] The ILP's anti-war stand was, however, not that of the majority of trade unionists of the time: indeed union agreement to suspend industrial action and wage claims for the duration of the war was an accomplished fact in Bristol even before the industrial truce was proclaimed nationally by the TUC and Labour Party.

However, while Asquith remained prime minister, the Trades Council's demand for effective price-control went largely unheard: prices continued to rise. There was little the Council could do but protest. In February 1915, for instance, it held a mass meeting to rally support for Labour MPs pressing for such control in the Commons.[53] Nothing was achieved; Asquith rejected state intervention and in effect told wage earners to grin and bear it. The upshot was predictable. The Trades Council's affiliated unions, faced with ever rising prices and ineffective government action, were in an ever-stronger bargaining position as the demand for labour to feed the war machine soared, and eventually they broke the industrial truce and demanded higher wages. The dockers led the way, obtaining a war bonus in March 1915[54] and by June the engineers, boot and shoe operatives, railwaymen, miners, furniture workers and bakers had all won increases. The industrial truce had broken down as became glaringly obvious when in May 1915 the workers at Douglas Bros., engaged in making vehicles for the army, ignoring a Kitchener-style appeal to speed up work, walked out on strike.[55] It was the first strike the city had known for ten months but the forerunner of many that followed a similar pattern: there was a spontaneous outburst by hitherto often unorganised workers against the refusal of anti-union employers to grant a wage increase to match rising prices.[56] Organised workers were winning their increases. The obvious moral was to organise, and this was where the general unions, the Gasworkers, the Workers' Union and, above all, the Dockers came in. Such unions rather than the Trades Council were very active in recruiting and organising the hitherto unorganised. The result was that such workers looked more to the ever-growing Dockers' Union than to the Council to express their aspirations effectively. Significantly, T.C. Lewis, the Council's secretary

52 Bristol ILP minutes, 10 August 1914.
53 *Western Daily Press*, 2 February 1915.
54 *Dockers' Record*, March 1915.
55 *Western Daily Press*, 4 May 1915.
56 The climax was reached in a series of strikes against the Tramway Co. whose managing director, Sir George Verdon-Smith, was regarded as the most violently anti-union employer in the city.

until 1917, a member of the Operative Bricklayer's Society, decided to resign and join the vigorous Dockers' Union. He quickly found himself an organiser with special responsibility for East Bristol, one of the fastest growing branches. By the end of the war the Dockers' Union probably contained as many members as *all* the unions of pre-war Bristol put together, and there was scarcely a trade or industry in the city that was not represented in some degree in it. Not surprisingly, such a giant union, held together not as craft unions were by common possession of a skill but by loyalty to a centralized leadership and class solidarity of its heterogeneous membership, tended to regard outside bodies such as the Council or rival general unions as threats to its own cohesion. Smaller unions complained to the Council that the Dockers poached on their preserves, but there was little it could do to prevent this any more than it was able to prevent the Dockers taking the lead on questions previously regarded as the Council's special concern. Two examples must suffice: in 1917 the Dockers ignored the Council when they convened a mass meeting to hear the minister, H.A.L. Fisher expound the principles of the Education Bill he was about to pilot through parliament.[57] Education questions had hitherto been regarded as Trades Council business rather than that of a single member union. Again, in the later stages of the war, it was Bevin in his capacity as National Organiser of the Dockers' Union, not as representative of the Trades Council, who led the campaigns against profiteering, especially in the food trade,[58] an issue which the Council thought it had made peculiarly its own.

The erosion of the Council's effectiveness during the war was also due to the mixture of impotence and militancy it displayed over the major issue of conscription. In June 1915 it sought to give a lead to the labour movement in the city by coming out unequivocally against conscription. Unhappily for the Council, opinion was much divided. The ILP whose influence was considerable in the Council, though extremely limited in the city itself, was firmly anti-conscriptionist. The ILP's chief spokesman, Walter Ayles, city councillor and office-holder in the Trades Council, was such a staunch objector that he was to serve on the No-Conscription Fellowship's national executive and end up in

57 *Western Daily Press*, 15 October 1917.
58 *Ibid.* 9 July 1917.

prison for his beliefs.[59] On the other hand some prominent unionists and Labour councillors, such as Whitfield, the miners' agent, and Frank Sheppard, were firmly 'patriotic' and supported the policy adopted by the TUC when it met in Bristol (for the third time) in September 1915 that every encouragement should be given to Lord Derby's voluntary recruiting scheme. It was the 'patriotic' group which made the running, issuing a *Bristol Trade Union Manifesto* warning that "The Empire is in danger from Prussian aggression", calling on unionists to volunteer and implying that if they did not it would be their own fault if conscription was introduced.[60] This was followed up in November 1915, with a recruiting rally in the Colston Hall addressed by 'patriotic' socialists such as the ex-Bristolians Ben Tillett and James O'Grady (Labour MP for Leeds) and Will Crooks.[61]

The Trades Council reacted by contradicting TUC policy. It declared neutrality towards the recruiting campaign and eventually under ILP pressure it proceeded to mount a campaign against conscription. But it left this until very late in the day, launching it when the bill was actually before parliament in January 1916 and, militant as some of the speeches were at the mass rally sponsored by the Trades Council, the practical upshot was nil.[62] Furthermore the Council, again much influenced by its ILP members, almost certainly further isolated itself from majority opinion in the Bristol labour movement by continuing to oppose conscription once it was the law of the land and by declaring in April 1916 that it would do all it could to help conscientious objectors. Brave though such a stand was, given the often brutal and hysterical response of authority to conscientious objectors, the truth was that if the Council did not want to lose support or prove its ineffectiveness there was only one policy on an issue as contentious as this and that was to say nothing, as Bevin realised. However, it is probable that the Council had no option but to take a stand and accept the consequences. If it had followed the totally different view of the ultra-patriotic Bristol branch of the Bristol Socialist Party, the result would probably have been the same.

59 WH Ayles (1879–1953) was the dominant figure in the ILP in the West country, serving as general secretary of the Bristol branch for 12 years and on the party's national administrative council. At this time, he was also President of the Bristol LRC. He was leader of the 'absolutist' wing of the No-Conscription Fellowship, refusing to undertake national service of *any* kind (for the Fellowship see D. Boulton, *Objection Overruled* (1967)). Later Ayles became Labour MP for Bristol North, 1923–4, 1929–31 and for Southall 1945–1950 and Hayes and Harlington 1950–53.
60 *Western Daily Press*, 26 October 1915.
61 *Western Daily Press*, 22 November 1915.
62 *Bristol Times and Mirror*, 17 January 1916.

Left: Arthur Dickinson, carter in Bristol docks and conscientious objector during the First World War. Right: Don Bateman.

Bristol Trades Council President, Don Bateman (DB), in conversation with Arthur Dickinson (AD) in 1973...

DB: "The First World War was a gigantic watershed for the working-class movements of Europe."

"Ernest Bevin, then a member of the Bristol Trades Council, first called for a General Strike against the War but spent the next four years building up his dockers union. Many of his members were influenced by the pro-war hysteria which was being fostered by the press. But a majority of the Trades Council opposed conscription. The Council was influenced in their stand by the strong internationalist attitude of the Independent Labour Party. Arthur Dickinson was a member of both, at the time a carter on Bristol docks and one of Bevin's lieutenants.

What were your personal feelings as a socialist in the 1914-18 War?"

AD: "Well my position was that I was a Sunday school teacher at that time and I felt that the New Testament taught me not to fight. So, I was a conscientious objector and whatever happened I wouldn't have went to war. So, I followed Bevin and we used to discuss these things at our branch meetings and very often we used to have some very strong discussions on it.

But right throughout the War, I supported the conscientious objectors and even after that I was still a conscientious objector."

DB: "Many conscientious objectors were lodged in Horfield prison. They were deprived of Bibles – clearly the authorities considered the New Testament a seditious document which would reinforce the philosophy of those opposed to pro-war propaganda.

Words on a poster at Douglas Brothers' Kingswood factory: "Now Mr Workman would you help Kitchener and your pal Tommy KICK THE KAISER. If so, it's up to you to put in as many hours in a day at the bench as possible. Think of what Tommy Atkins is doing in the trenches and think too that your bench is a trench. Come on—we know you're British but show Kitchener you're British, aye British, right to the backbone!"

DB: "And within 24 hours of the posters going up in the factory, the Kingswood workers were all out on strike."

AD: "We were all amazed by the situation and, seeing some of the fellows that came back, we felt more than ever against the war."

Finally, in the closing year of the war far-reaching changes in the organisation of the labour movement occurred. The Labour Party's 1918 constitution abolished Labour Representation Committees (LRCs) in which Trades Councils had often been highly influential. In Bristol, for instance, in 1914, the President of the Council was also President of the LRC. Instead, there were established local Labour parties at constituency and ward level which in the 'coupon' election in December 1918 contested four out of five Bristol parliamentary seats, though without success.[63] In addition, the Bristol Borough Labour Party was set up as a central coordinating body, with delegations from local ward and constituency parties, affiliated trade unions, and political societies, and with responsibility for deciding policy in municipal affairs. In effect, the Trades Council lost most of its previous political function and the new arrangement imposed an organisational separation on the political and trade union wings of the movement.

Almost immediately, however, the Trades Council and Borough Labour Party began discussions on the question of fusion. As the central coordinating bodies of different wings of the same movement, a wasteful duplication of effort, if not friction, would have been unavoidable had the two bodies maintained an entirely separate existence. In 1919, therefore they set up a Fusion Committee, and the following year adopted its recommendation that henceforth they should be known as the *Bristol Trades and Labour Council,* employing a single full-time secretary, and using the same headquarters, but retaining separate executives and delegate meetings.[64] Edwin Parker, a member of the Dockers' Union, was elected first secretary of the new body, and he continued to serve in this capacity throughout the inter-war period, until illness forced him to retire in 1942. The fusion survived under his secretaryship, but increasingly since the Second World War, the two bodies have developed an independent existence.

Changes in the trade union world, as well as in the Labour Party, also impinged upon the functions of Trades Councils at this time. The growth of national rather than local collective bargaining and the increasing centralisation of authority within individual unions reduced the scope for local initiative. Trade Councils, since they linked workers in various unions and different industries, cut across the lines of authority in individual unions. Hence union national executives have,

63 Labour contested Bristol North, South, East and Central constituencies. Ernest Bevin was candidate in the latter.
64 BTC papers in the City Archives.

for the most part, opposed extensions of their functions, or at least insisted on a clear definition of their role. Since 1924, the TUC's General Council has sought to integrate the Trades Councils into the changed structure of the trade union movement—by, for example, sponsoring an annual conference of Trades Councils and seeking to use Councils as its local agents. They have headed off the threat to the authority of national executives of individual unions, which is implicit in the structure of Trades Councils, by restricting their representation at the TUC Annual Congress to a single fraternal delegate, and by seeking to control their activities by drawing up a register of recognised Councils which conformed to the General Council's conception of what their rules and functions should be.

In the inter-war period, the Bristol Trades and Labour Council adapted itself to changed circumstances. On what might loosely be called the political side of its work, it sought to take advantage of the practice, increasingly evident from the war onwards, of co-opting Labour representation on to a variety of official and semi-public bodies to put the trade union point of view. Industrially, in the twenties and early thirties, the main concerns of the Council were the maintenance of union membership and the rallying of support for unionists involved in disputes.

One of the most important functions of the Council was to organise campaigns in association with the officials of local unions. From time to time the Council would act as the local agent of the TUC during national campaigns aimed at specific groups of workers among whom trade unionism was weak, such as women workers. Other campaigns were the result of local initiative and aimed at specifically local 'blackspots'. Immediately after the war union membership reached an all-time high, but with the onset of the depression in 1921, with consequent heavy and persistent unemployment, union membership fell sharply, especially amongst groups of workers where there was no long tradition of trade unionism. The position of the unions in the tobacco factories, for instance, suffered a severe setback; whilst on the tramways, unionism was virtually eradicated in 1923. All unions lost heavily. The TGWU (heir to the Dockers' Union) which in 1921 claimed 40,000 members in Bristol[65] had shrunk to a mere 12,000 in 1928.[66]

With workers leaving the unions at such a rate, there was little that the Council could do to stem the tide. It did, however, try to co-ordinate

65 *Western Daily Press*, 24 October 1921.
66 TGWU *Annual Report*, 1928.

During the General Strike of 1926, the BTC took on a key role in organising local support.

and encourage the efforts of the various unions to recoup their losses. Workers in the printing trades attracted the attention of the Council's recruiting drive in 1925–6, while in 1927 a campaign was aimed at the tobacco factories, but success was limited. The women's tobacco worker branch of the TGWU had shrunk from a membership of almost 2,900 in 1922 to 737 in 1927. Despite the campaign, membership of the branch continued to fall, there being 425 members in 1928.[67] It was only when employment prospects improved in the mid-thirties that the Council's efforts met with some success and union membership once more began to climb.

The years 1919–1926 witnessed unprecedentedly bitter struggles between Capital and Labour. The sacrifices demanded of workers during the war prompted them to press their demands for a better, more secure standard of living in the post-war world with exceptional militancy. Socialist ideas gained a greater currency than ever before. In 1921, however, the post-war boom collapsed, turned into a slump, and mass

67 TGWU *Annual Reports passim.*

unemployment established itself as a permanent feature of the inter-war years. The slump brought in its train demands from employers, often enforced through lock-out, for wage reductions. All the gains won in the previous period by the unions were now threatened. Strikes and lockouts, both local and national, were frequently prolonged and fought with determination and bitterness on both sides. Several times the Council was called upon to organise support for unionists in dispute. On occasion this was of a moral kind, as when during the 1924 national railway engine drivers' strike the Council and ASLEF jointly arranged a meeting to put the strikers' case before the public.[68] Sometimes financial help was given as in the mining lock-out of 1921 when the Council raised over £1,000 for the Bristol miners.[69]

During the 1926 General Strike, however, the Council was called upon to play a much more important and active role. Indeed, this had been prefigured a year earlier when the miners faced the threat of wage cuts for the second time in four years and called on the TUC for support. Throughout the trade union movement there was tremendous sympathy for the miners' cause and a readiness to take action in support, for the defeat of the miners in 1921 had been the prelude to wage cutting throughout industry. A further defeat for the miners would weaken the resistance of the whole union movement to another round of wage cuts. This had been the view of the Trades Council in 1921, expressed by its secretary, E.H. Parker. "The present critical industrial situation", he wrote, "is caused by an attempt on the part of organised capitalism to establish a right of unlimited plunder. It must be resisted at all costs, for it is not only an attack on the miners but the beginning of an offensive against the standard of life of the whole community".[70] Thus when, in 1925, the miners called on the TUC for support in their resistance to wage reductions, the Council prepared for action. In the event of sympathetic action being called by the TUC's General Council, Trades Councils were to act as local organising centres passing on instructions to local trade unionists. On July 31, 'Red Friday', a special delegate meeting of the Bristol Trades Council was convened at the request of the TUC to discuss plans for the strike. At the last moment the government backed down and granted the coal industry a subsidy to enable it to continue paying the old wages for a further nine months. A telegram announcing this news and declaring the strike off arrived during the course of the Council meeting.

68 *Western Daily Press*, 28 January 1924.
69 *Western Daily Press*, 21 May 1921.
70 *Western Daily Press*, 16 April 1921.

Ron Whiteford interviewing Bill Paxton—still from '*100 Years of Struggle*'.

Ron Whiteford (RW), Trades Council representative for the Amalgamated Engineering Union:

"Britain in 1926 was not the land fit for heroes that had been promised. The mineworkers were in the vanguard, then as now, and were prepared to take on the state to stop cuts in their wages."

BBC announcement: We regret to have to announce that all efforts at compromise between the Trades Union Council and the government on the coal mines having failed, a General Strike will begin at midnight.

RW: "At the coalfields on May 4th, pickets were on duty but none were needed. Railways and docks were paralysed for workers took up the call to stop work enthusiastically. It was the greatest confrontation ever seen between employers and their government and the employees. In Bristol the Trades Council set up a central strike committee of which Bill Paxton was a member. As an engine driver, he was also a member of the railway sub-committee whose job it was to keep control of the situation."

RW in conversation with engine driver Bill Paxton (BP):

BP: "It was the finest experience I ever had in real revolutionary work. We had control of all the meat, all the supplies from the goods sheds and they had to come to us if we would allow so-and-so to come out."

RW: "You had really the power and control."

BP: "We had the power and control. We had real power."

RW: "Temple Meads came to a standstill. In Bristol only the trams continued to run. Trade union organisation on the trams had been smashed before the strike began. The failure of the strike on the tramways did not deter other workers. Although Bristol papers still appeared full of anti-strike propaganda, the government was visibly shaken when production stopped on such a vast scale. In Bristol eighteen thousand workers had come out immediately and by May 11th that figure had nearly doubled. Some of the sons and daughters of the upper class turned their hand to the novelty of work. Students from Bristol University moved supplies. The army and police were brought in to provide protection against angry workers for tension built up when blacklegs came to the aid of the capitalist state. Then, despite the solidarity of the working class and their determination to win...".

BBC announcement: This is London calling the British Isles. We have just received the news that the General Strike has been called off by the leaders of the Trades Union Council.

BP: "The news came through. That was twelve days—it had been called off. You've never seen such unbelievable expressions on men's faces. We were on the peak of victory. We were touching the plum on top of the tree."

The crisis had been postponed. During the period of the nine-month subsidy the Government made extensive preparation to meet a General Strike. And when in May 1926 the government refused to renew the subsidy but insisted that the miners should accept wage reductions, the miners called on the TUC to carry out the threatened General Strike. On 3rd May the stoppage began. Workers everywhere responded to the strike call with enthusiasm and determination. On the first day in Bristol 18,000 workers downed tools; nine days later, just before the strike was called off, that number had doubled.[71] Among local miners, dockers, transport workers and railwaymen the strike was solid from the beginning. These groups were joined by others as the General Strike spread: electrical power station workers, builders, printers and engineers coming out in the course of the nine days, while yet other groups of workers were waiting for the call when the order to return to work was received. Although the tramways and the local press managed to continue operations, the major industries of the town were effectively brought to a halt, and despite the show of force by the Government—warships were moved into the Avonmouth and City Docks and sailors guarded the power station— there was no sign of weakening while the strike lasted.

With such a large number of workers on strike and awaiting instructions the role of the Council was crucial. Before May the Council, like the TUC at national level, had made no detailed plans for the strike, and it was not until the evening of 3rd May, only hours before the strike was due to begin, that delegates met to discuss local organisation. Nevertheless, despite their unpreparedness Bristol unionists showed the same capacity for spontaneous self-organisation which characterised the strike in several localities. The meeting on 3rd May decided to set up a Central Strike Committee representing the Council and those unions involved. This was to be in session day and night and to be responsible for conveying messages and instructions from the General Council to the rank and file and was to transmit information about the position in Bristol to strike headquarters. Special sub-committees were established to deal with communications and publicity, the latter issuing regular strike bulletins. A system of cyclist messengers was devised for carrying information speedily from the centre to all points of the city.[72] The system seems to have worked well, and though some delay and confusion was experienced in the issuing of strike orders to some workers, this did not hamper the general effectiveness of the strike.

71 *TUC Library* (HD5336) General Strike, local reports.
72 *Western Daily Press*, 4 May 1926.

Hence when on 12th May the TUC unconditionally called off the General Strike, the news was received in Bristol with a mixture of shock, anger and dismay. There seemed no apparent reason why the unions should accept defeat: the local Amalgamated Engineering Union (AEU) official observed later that "We were in a strong position on the 12th."[73] At first the assumption was that the unions must have won a victory. When it became clear that the TUC had accepted defeat, the reaction was one of protest, followed by demoralisation. The miners fought on alone but they too were eventually beaten. In December, after a lock-out lasting seven months, the exhausted and penniless Bristol miners were forced back to work on the employers' terms of reduced wages and longer hours. The trade unions emerged from the General Strike as a movement in retreat. Many employers used their position of strength to impose new and more onerous terms on unionists who had taken part in the strike, and to curb the future activities of the unions. In the next few years, the Council was but rarely called upon to organise support for unionists in dispute for a strike was a very rare occurrence in Bristol.

Between the wars, the Council's attention was directed increasingly to the struggle of the unemployed. Even in 1919, at the height of the post-war boom, large numbers of ex-servicemen were unable to find work. Many of them joined organisations specifically for ex-servicemen, some of which tended to blame the unions for the unemployment of their members. Craft restrictions on the number of apprentices, for example, came under attack as being allegedly practices which caused unemployment. And the continued employment of women on the trams, after the war, led to physical attacks on tramcars and the company offices by ex-servicemen demanding that these jobs be given to men. After several such attacks in April 1920, the Tramways Company agreed to the ex-servicemen's demands.[74]

The Council's attitude at this time was one of sympathy with the demand for work or for full maintenance, mixed with suspicion of the aims and methods of the ex-servicemen's organisations. During 1919 and 1920, when these bodies had leadership over the local agitation, the Council tended to hold aloof, and thus to confirm the suspicion of many ex-servicemen that the trade unions were indifferent to their cause. This attitude, however, carried with it severe dangers. At the municipal elections in 1919, the ex-servicemen's organisations put up nine candidates, eight of them in direct opposition to Labour candidates,

73 AEU *Monthly Report.*
74 *Western Daily Press*, 27–29 April 1920.

thus threatening to split the working-class vote. For the trade unions there was the very real danger, in a period of intense industrial conflict, that vast reserves of unemployed workers, hostile to the unions, might be recruited to break strikes. In fact, unionists on strike were always careful to form links with the unemployed and thus minimise the risk, but the threat remained.

The policy of aloofness from the struggles of the unemployed was very much that of the TUC. The early unemployed organisations tried repeatedly to press the TUC into taking on the responsibility for directing the struggle but without success.[75] But at a local level, aloofness was proving increasingly untenable. In 1921 unemployment increased rapidly and trade union membership suffered. In the same year, the special post-war donation benefit was ended and the unemployed, if they were ineligible for Unemployment Insurance benefit, had to apply to the local Board of Guardians for outdoor relief. The unemployed themselves were beginning to adopt a more militant stance, demanding the raising of relief scales by the Guardians. In September 1921, after a series of demonstrations and baton charges by the police outside the Guardians offices in St Peter's Hospital, the relief scales were raised.

In 1920 and 1921 the Trades Council began to take a more active role in the organisation of the unemployed, attempting to formulate a policy that would link them with those still in employment. A Bristol Unemployed Association (BUA), affiliated to the Trades Council, was set up in 1921 and this body, although not formally under the control of the Council, did provide the vehicle by which the Council wrested control of the local unemployed movement from the militants. Its secretary, E.H. Parker, was also the Trades and Labour Council Secretary, and its organiser, J. Linton, was a former leader of the ex-servicemen. The BUA, in the months and years following the violent clashes of 1920–21, steered the movement away from physical confrontation with the police and into constitutional channels. The correct way to fight unemployment, it argued, was through the ballot box by the election of a Labour government at Westminster and a Labour council in Bristol. Deputations to the Board of Guardians, and occasionally to the City Council, were still a feature of its work, but without the accompanying march and demonstration at the gates of St Peter's Hospital. Indeed, one of the first demands formulated by the BUA in 1921 was for the unemployed to be given the use of halls for their meetings so that

75 W Hannington, *Unemployed Struggles* (1936).

they had no need to meet on the streets and so risk a clash with the police. The Guardians themselves were very grateful to the BUA when, in October 1922, the Board called in the police to protect their offices during a meeting, in the fear that the militants were re-establishing their influence and planning a demonstration. The Chairman of the Board hastened to express his gratitude to Messrs. Parker and Linton who "had been very valuable in keeping the men in check".[76] The Council was active in pressing the claims of the unemployed and in formulating schemes of work to absorb them back into employment but, in the hardening climate of retrenchment, it was able to win very few concessions. A scheme prepared by the Council to take over from the Guardians the contract for cutting a new road at Southmead, and so employ a large number of unemployed, whilst still paying full trade union rates, was turned down flat.[77]

The unemployed struggle tended to subside somewhat after 1923, though the BUA and the Council continued to work together. In 1927 a major reorganisation was instituted, when the BUA was taken directly under the wing of the Council. At the same time, a more precise formulation of aims was issued: the objects of the Association were stated to be "to combine in one organisation the employed and unemployed for combatting the evils arising from unemployment, to impress upon the Government and local authorities the need for providing work, and to obtain for the unemployed persons as high a standard of living as possible, and the inauguration of schemes which will prevent the degradation of those who are workless and their dependants".[78]

In part the Association functioned as an organising auxiliary to the trade union movement. Members were issued with a membership card, similar to any trade union 'ticket', and this was interchangeable with an appropriate union card when the holder found employment. It was on this basis that the trade unions, which had long approached the question of an independent unemployed organisation with considerable reserve, gave their support and financial backing to the scheme. They were well rewarded. In 1932 it was reported that the BUA had, since 1927, turned over at least 700 members to local union branches.[79]

76 *Bristol Times and Mirror*, 28 October 1922.
77 *Western Daily Press*, 16 January 1922.
78 *Bristol Times and Mirror*, 2 February 1928.
79 TUC *Congress Report*, 1932 p.123.

As a trade union for the unemployed, the BUA sought recognition from the authorities of its right to negotiate on their behalf. This recognition was granted, and annual reports of the Trades Council from the period tell of the work of the Association in "handling many hundreds of individual cases with the Public Assistance Committee, at Courts of Referees, and rent and rate cases." A major part of its work, however, was concerned with unemployed welfare. This is reflected in the composition of its committee of management which included representatives not only of the Trades Council and the unemployed themselves, but also representatives of the Christian churches, city councillors and members of the Board of Guardians. Increasing emphasis was placed on the educational and welfare side of its work, with weekly public speaker meetings, and an annual outing for the children of the unemployed paid for by public appeal.

The scheme was very successful in enrolling the unemployed of Bristol in membership. Branches were set up in various parts of the city; within six months there were already four branches and later more were added, including two for unemployed women. Indeed, the BUA was so successful that the TUC considered adopting the scheme and sponsoring similar associations in other towns. At the 1928 Annual Congress the General Council reported that, "Arising out of the success attained by the Bristol Trades Council in organising unemployed workers in an association under the direct auspices of the Council, the Trades Councils Joint Consultative Committee gave consideration to the possibility of extending the scheme." The General Council recommended to Congress that an experimental scheme be launched on the Bristol lines in six towns. Congress, however, was not convinced and referred the proposal back.[80] Several Trades Councils, on their own initiative, did study the Bristol scheme and start similar associations in their towns and, in 1932, the whole question again came before the TUC, which agreed to take over responsibility for this type of unemployed organisation, and ratified a model constitution for the guidance of Trades Councils.[81]

The local unemployment index for the years 1928–1939 shows that even though Bristol suffered less unemployment than the national average, and certainly less than many of the northern industrial cities, the rate was high by any standard. Among insured adult male workers there was not at any time less than 10 percent unemployment in the

80 TUC *Congress Report*, 1932 p.111.
81 TUC *Congress Report*, 1932 p. 121.

years 1928–1937, and during the worst years of the slump, in 1931–1933, the rate was well over 20 per cent, with a peak in March 1932 of 24.5 per cent.[82] Moreover, in 1931, with the formation of the National Government, relief scales came under attack and means tests were introduced, in an effort to cut government expenditure. In response, the struggles of the unemployed became more intense, and the BUA found its leadership of the local unemployed challenged with increasing success by the more militant National Unemployed Workers' Movement (NUWM). During 1932 to 1934, the latter body made the running. The unemployed again appeared on the streets in force, marches and demonstrations backing up deputations to the City Council or Public Assistance Committee (PAC). In September 1931 the NUWM led a march, not to the City Council but to the TUC, which was meeting at the time in Bristol. The Congress, as in former years, refused to admit the deputation. Frequently these marches came into conflict with the police. Baton charges were used against the unemployed in September 1931, and on five separate occasions in 1932. The *Bristol Evening Post* described one such incident in June 1932, thus:

DEMONSTRATORS AMBUSHED BY POLICE IN CASTLE STREET

In a police charge in Castle St. shortly before 10.30 there were seventy casualties and twenty-nine people were treated for more or less serious injuries. The scene was a remarkable one. It was just between the lights and as the electric streetlamps came on just after the charge was made, the street looked like a battlefield. Men lay prone in every direction and blood ran on the pavements…

Just what precipitated the trouble is not clear, but suddenly there emerged from side streets and shop doorways a strong body of police reinforcements with batons drawn. They set about clearing the streets. Men fell right and left under their charge, and women who got mixed up in the crowd were knocked down in the wild rush to escape. The cries of men and terrified shrieking of women added to the tumult. Then came a troop of mounted police charging through Castle Street from

82 *Ministry of Labour Statistics Division, Local Employment Index.*

Ellis Justan, St John's ambulanceman who witnessed the 1932 police attack.

Ellis Justan (pictured) was an ambulanceman on 9th June 1932...

Ron Whiteford: "Instead of the system being changed, the ugly face of capitalism became worse with mounting unemployment. The struggles of the unemployed culminating in the hunger marches of the 30s. Bristol Trades Council was appalled by the outcome of a demonstration on June 9th 1932."

Bill Paxton: "It was a demonstration against the Means Test and also for extra winter coal of half a hundred weight. About fifteen thousand took part in the demonstration which started from the Horsefair, moving round Trinity Church, and entered Old Market and reached the point over there." (pointing across Old Market.)

EJ: (standing in Old Market) "They met a body of policemen here who turned them back."

RW: "Ellis Justan, now a member of Bristol Trades Council, was then a St John's ambulanceman at the scene.

EJ: "The order was given to clear the streets."

BP: "The police charged. They came from the Drill Hall over there. They came from the Caxton Hall, I was told, they came from there. They came from what was Carey's Lane, from the Tower Hill area and they cut the leadership – of which I was one – of the demonstration away from the rest. It was one of the most vicious attacks possible on the working class."

EJ: "I saw some very odd things. There was a lamp post over there, a man running round it at a tremendous speed. I think he thought he was running away."

BP: "There were cries and screams. The banners were smashed by the police. The whole thing was like a battlefield."

the Old Market End scattering the last of the demonstrators. In a few minutes the streets were clear, save the men who lay with cracked heads groaning on the pavements and in shop doorways where they had staggered for refuge.[83]

The Council joined in the chorus of protest from the Bristol Labour movement at this attack. But its link with the unemployed had been considerably weakened. On the one hand, the BUA had to compete for leadership of the local unemployed with the NUWM, an uphill task in the years 1931–1934. But also, the secretaryship of the BUA had been resigned by Parker in 1931 and taken over by Councillor Berriman, the secretary of the Bristol ILP.[84] While the Trades Council was still involved in the organisation of the unemployed, its activity in this question was increasingly a matter of political action through public protest meetings organised jointly with the Labour Party, and through the work of Labour councillors on the City Council. But the organisation of the unemployed themselves could not be ignored. It was the marches and deputations in 1932 which forced the City Council to delay the operation of the PAC relief cuts for six months. The means test was the subject of a continuous agitation, as was the test work system—the practice of forcing the unemployed men applying for assistance to undertake test or task work,

83 *Bristol Evening Post*, 10 June 1932.
84 *Bristol ILP Minutes*, May 1931.

at very low wages, in order to prove their availability for employment. In August 1933, some 250 test workers took strike action.[85] The Trades Council, the BUA and the NUWM were all active in organising the strike and putting pressure on the City Council to abolish the system of test work. But association with this more militant action placed the Council in something of a dilemma. The test-work strikers decided in September to send a deputation to the 1933 Trades Union Congress to demand that it support their cause. If the Council had been implicated in this action it would have come into conflict with the TUC which had consistently refused to receive unemployed deputations. Rather than allow this to happen the Council's secretary abandoned the cause of the test workers and withdrew from the strike committee.[86] The strike collapsed two weeks later.

During 1934 and 1935 the BUA and NUWM maintained separate agitations on the unemployment question. By this time, however, economic activity was beginning to pick up and unemployment was on the decline. The campaign in 1935 against Part II of the 1934 Unemployment Insurance Act was the last major protest by the unemployed in Bristol. In 1937 the local rate of unemployment dipped below 10 per cent and although it crept up again to over 11 per cent in mid-1938, the general trend was downwards. By June the rate had fallen to 6.3 per cent.

One of the major factors in the recovery was the pre-war rearmament, and this was particularly true of the Bristol region, with major aircraft factories situated at Filton, Patchway and Yate. These factories underwent an enormous expansion in the years immediately preceding the war, thus opening wider employment opportunities. The Council, however, believed that this employment was "necessarily of a temporary character".[87] Rearmament, moreover, implied a growing threat of war, and this threat, and the need to define its attitude to it, increasingly preoccupied the Council in the late 1930s. Ever since 1918, the Council had allied itself with anti-war groups. In August 1920, following the TUC's initiative in establishing a Council of Action to organise strikes against any attempt by the British Government to intervene in the Russo-Polish war on the side of the Poles, a Trades Council local Action Committee was set up.[88] During the 1920s the Council was an

85 *Western Daily Press*, 1 August 1933.
86 *Western Daily Press*, 4 September 1933.
87 BTC *Statement of Accounts*, 1936.
88 *Western Daily Press*, 23 August 1920.

enthusiastic supporter of the League of Nations Movement and one of the main sponsors behind the Bristol No-More-War Movement, which united all pacifist and anti-war groups. Later, a Bristol Peace Council was formed, uniting the Council with Labour, socialist, and other political and religious groups whose common denominator was aversion to war.

The victory of fascism in Italy and Germany, and its rise in Spain, was seen by the Trades Council as a clear threat to the international working-class movement. It created a situation in which pacifism was seen as inappropriate. A significant section of the Bristol Labour movement advocated with increasing force, from 1936 onwards, an independent working-class response to the fascist threat, based on a United Front of all socialist, labour and co-operative organisations. The Trades Council's 1934 Annual Report speaks of its active assistance to a movement against fascism in Britain. After the outbreak of the Spanish Civil War, the Council agitated on behalf of the Republican cause, and advocated that Britain should supply arms and active assistance to the Republicans. But, in line with official Labour and TUC policy, the Council refused to associate itself with the campaign for a United Front, or with the later Popular Front campaign.

During 1938 and 1939, war seemed at all times imminent. The Trades Council's response was somewhat confused. On the one hand, it was still affiliated to the predominantly pacifist Bristol Peace Council. But on the other hand, it advocated increasingly, a firmer stand against Hitler, and an end to appeasement. When Chamberlain negotiated his notorious 'peace with honour' at Munich in September 1938, the Council unequivocally condemned the settlement as being one which would make war inevitable. A resolution passed by a full delegate meeting expressed its "abhorrence of the betrayal of Czechoslovakia by the British Prime Minister and his Cabinet" and called upon the British Labour movement "to offer every opposition to the proposed destruction of the Czechoslovakia state".[89] In the Council's view, a firm stand was necessary. Because of its absolute distrust of the Chamberlain Government especially after Munich, the Council opposed its preparations for war, such as conscription. But its opposition was somewhat equivocal, since war was clearly implicit in the Council's demand for further action. The alternative—an independent working-class policy of opposition to fascism—was one the Council refused to adopt.

89 *Bristol Evening Post*, 22 September 1930.

When war was finally declared in September 1939, the Trades Council accepted the inevitability of the situation and adopted the role it had sought to perform during the First World War of watchdog over working-class interests. Within days of the conflict beginning the joint executives of the Trades Council and Borough Labour Party set up Vigilance Committees in the wards and parliamentary divisions to watch out for profiteering and distress.[90] As refugees arrived from the continent the Council offered them help, collecting and distributing money. For the most part the Council continued its routine work during the war despite the destruction of its offices in the air raid of 1941. But the war also led to a shift of emphasis in its activity. On the one hand, disputes were infrequent and always unofficial, since the trade union leaders had agreed not to use the strike weapon. Unemployment all but disappeared. Trade union recruitment was important, and indeed the unions grew at a rapid rate, yet while Trades Council support was a valuable asset in any recruiting campaign undertaken by the unions, the difficulties that had previously stood in the way of union growth had been removed by war-time conditions. Hence there was very little scope for Trades Council activity in those areas which had traditionally attracted its attention.

On the other hand, trade union support for the war effort was assiduously cultivated, especially after the formation of the 'National' Government in 1940, which included Ernest Bevin as Minister of Labour. Increasingly during the war trade unionists were co-opted on to official committees to represent the trade union point of view and to tie the unions more closely to the war effort. The Council's job was to nominate suitable candidates for such posts. E.V. Rees who took over as Trades Council secretary after Parker suffered a stroke in 1942 recalls that he served on no less than 22 such committees during the war. Apart from the Council's involvement in Air Raid Precautions (ARP) work and in recruiting campaigns for the forces, it was also represented on various committees set up by the Ministry of Information and the Ministry of Labour, on bodies concerned with increasing production, and was involved in the mechanics of rationing. Mr. Rees, for example, was charged with the responsibility for distributing petrol rations to the trade unions in the South West Region.[91]

Doubtless it was the enhanced importance of the Council which was responsible for the increase in the proportion of local unions

90 Bristol South Divisional Labour Party, *Minutes*, September 1939
91 Conversation with the author.

Ernest Bevin, Bristol dockers leader
and later war-time Minister of Labour.

Bristol Post Office workers on the march, May Day 1947.

Ron Whiteford addressing the BTC in 1973.

In 1973, Ron Whiteford described how the Trades Council was vigorously opposed to the rundown of engineering in Bristol and was in angry mood when it debated a proposal by Mike Berry of ASTMS for discontinuing TUC talks with the government.

Mike Berry speaking at the Bristol Trades Council meeting: "This is not a motion that says there should be no negotiation with anybody on any question and that's not an issue. And there is no attempt on my part to say that there should be no negotiation with the government of the day. What I am saying is, and what I think this motion is saying, is that where you have a situation of the restriction of collective bargaining, the restriction of the trade union to pursue independent policies, it seems to me that involvement in that kind of negotiation can only compromise you from the word go."

A few delegates at the meeting opposed the motion, especially Albert Gospel.

Albert Gospel: "And if we talk of hamstringing our representative in the corridors of power, we must be very short-sighted in these days. We fought for a hundred years for the right to get near these people, to be given a hearing. If we are going to hamstring the people who represent us at the highest possible level, then we are fools. The day of trade unionism is come to a very low ebb. We can't go thumping the table with our cloth caps on, these days have gone. We've got to talk; we've got to make people listen to us."

A view Ron Whiteford was against…

"We all know that we have to negotiate with management on the shop-floor level. But there sometimes comes the point where it's important to get down with the lads and out of that board room with the management and take some action on the shop floor, then get something done. The management never mind you talking as much as you like, as long as there's no action at the end of it. We are having no truck with a government that actually imprisons people*. They have brought in laws to smash the trade unions and it's all very well, the argument isn't that they don't go away—no, but they get pretty ineffective!"

*On July 21ˢᵗ, 1972, five trade unionists were imprisoned on the orders of the Industrial Tribunal Court. Bristol Trades Council, like Councils throughout the country, called protest meetings and thousands of workers came out on strike. On July 26ᵗʰ the Pentonville Five were released.

affiliated to it. In 1945 an unprecedentedly high 95 per cent was claimed. Announcing this at the 1945 annual meeting, the Council's President G. Bullock drew the attention of the assembled delegates of the problems and potentialities of the approaching peace, which he greeted as heralding a new era. He expressed the opinion that the coming year "might prove the most momentous in the history of mankind", for they were about to lay the foundations of a lasting peace and a social system where unemployment was abolished and poverty exterminated.[92]

Since it was an integral part of the labour movement, the Council was expected to show loyalty to the policy of the Labour Party at Westminster and the labour-controlled City Council. Moreover, some of its officers and delegates were themselves councillors and therefore shared responsibility for these policies. Councillor G. Bullock, for

92 *Western Daily Press*, 16 February 1945.

example, who was Council President in 1944, 1945, 1949 and 1950 was also vice-chairman of the Housing Committee.[93] On the other hand, as the body representing the trade union wing of the movement, the Council did have an independent voice, and criticism of the policies of the Labour government was expressed through delegate meetings. Indeed, so apparently worried was the Borough Labour Party by this that at a meeting in October 1947 it disassociated itself from Trades Council criticisms which, it said, were the work of a minority of Communist delegates.[94] But, for the most part, opposition arose outside the Trades Council and the traditional channels of the labour movement. In particular, on the issue of Council house rents the campaign of opposition seems hardly to have involved the Trades Council at all and was instead led by a body known as the Bristol Council House Tenants' Defence Association.[95]

During the past quarter of a century the Trades Council has continued to be active in the role which previous developments had marked out for it. It continued to strive to maintain itself as the voice of the city's trade unionists as a whole on those matters which were not the immediate responsibility either of the individual unions or the political wing of the movement, while maintaining close relations with both. The Annual Report of 1967–1968 best expressed the Council's own view of itself and its functions by saying that it was not much concerned with the narrow area of the working day but with the "total environment affecting working people: at work; travelling; in health and sickness; in school and in the home; in leisure and recreation." At the same time the Council has sought to act as an educational influence on its members by arranging for expert speakers to address its monthly meetings, and among a wider audience has sought to propagate the philosophy of the trade union movement. The Bristol TUC 100 Festival in 1968, organised by the Council in association with local unions, was nationally recognised as being one of the most successful of its kind in the country.

Organisationally speaking, however, if the Council was to command attention, as it consistently realised, it must strive to speak as the representative body of all trade unionists in the city. This meant trying to achieve 100 per cent affiliation to it of local union branches and good attendance of delegates at monthly meetings. Success was by no means achieved in either respect. Annual Reports year after year

93 Conversation with the author.
94 *Bristol Evening Post*, 10 October 1947.
95 *Western Daily Press*, 8 June 1948.

express concern at the consistently low attendance of delegates, and at the dropping off in affiliations of important sections of the union movement. Branches of the AEU, for example, have long had a poor record in this respect. During the 1930s there were never more than two and frequently only one of the twelve or more local engineers' branches affiliated. By the 1950s this number had increased, but the eight affiliated branches of 1957 had fallen to four by 1959, despite the fact that in the major engineering dispute of 1957 the Council raised a considerable sum of money for the strikers. The number of AEU branches affiliated has remained consistently low since then.[96]

In part this gap in Trades Council membership reflects changes within the trade union movement. In an earlier period, it was the growth of national collective bargaining and the increasing centralisation of unions which detracted from the importance of Trades Councils. But the post-war world has witnessed the growth of increasingly powerful centrifugal forces within some unions, particularly in the engineering industry in which the workplace has replaced the geographically based branch as the centre of trade union activity, and shop-floor bargaining by shop stewards has taken over much of the work of the national negotiations. Since Trades Councils are precluded from establishing direct organisational links with shop stewards, the return of collective bargaining to the workplace has not been accompanied by an enhancing of the importance of the Councils. The basis of affiliation to the Council is the union branch, where branches are based on the workplace, as is increasingly the case in some unions, and where they maintain an active branch life, the Council is able through its affiliates to keep its links with the vital centres of trade union activity. But the decline of branch life in some unions and its replacement by workshop-based organisations with which the Council has no direct link, must ultimately detract from the importance of the Council.

Nevertheless, the continuing relevance of the Trades Council is demonstrated by the fact that it has been able to secure the affiliations of union branches, often in white-collar organisations, as these unions have themselves increasingly become affiliated to the TUC. The growth of white-collar trade unionism has been a striking feature of the last twenty-five years, and more and more of these organisations have expressed their identification with the working-class movement by affiliating to the Trades Council. In the sixties in particular this trend

96 Bristol Trades Council Annual Reports *passim.*

brought an infusion of new blood into the Council as, for example, teachers and workers in the media began to play a part in its affairs.

From time to time during the post-war period the Council has expressed opposition in a variety of ways to Government policies that it felt to be abhorrent. In 1956, for example, Council delegates joined with the rest of the labour movement in protesting against the invasion of Suez by British and French forces.[97] Unemployment, though for the most part not a serious threat to living standards for twenty years after the war, has recently returned to the scene, evoking memories of the 1930s, and drawing from the Council condemnations of economic policies which it regarded as responsible for the situation. In opposition to both the Labour Government's 'In Place of Strife' legislation, and to the Industrial Relations Act, the Council joined with the whole of trade union movement, and particularly in regard to the latter used its resources to explain to local trade union members the implications of the legislation for the movement.

The Council, however, has not confined its attentions to the immediate interests of local union members. Three examples from 1971 illustrate this fact. During the year the Council led a campaign in Bristol to bring to light the conditions of acute poverty and distress prevailing at a local Salvation Army hostel and demanded better accommodation for those who were forced to rely on such facilities. At the same time the Council provided two object lessons in international trade union solidarity. As an expression of sympathy with the plight of oppressed and poorly paid black South African coal miners, the Council used its links with local railwaymen to prevent a consignment of South African coal being imported through the port of Bristol. For this gesture of solidarity, a member of the South African Congress of Trade Unions conveyed the thanks to the delegates. Later in the same year an organiser from the United Farm Workers of America (UFWU) told a monthly meeting of a strike in California of immigrant grape-pickers for union recognition and higher pay and appealed to the Council for support. As a result, a picket was placed outside a local restaurant which had trading links with the American company involved. International pressure such as this was said by the UFWU, in a letter to the Council, to have contributed to the ultimate victory of the strike.

Throughout the past hundred years the Trades Council has sought to give expression to the views of trade unionists and to organise support

97 Bristol Trades Council *Annual Report 1956–7.*

The Bristol Bus Boycott forced the local Transport and General Workers Union to end the racist stand taken by its members, a stand criticised at the BTC's May Day rally in 1963. This mural, at Bristol bus station, is by Mike Baker.

for the members of unions involved in disputes. It is still actively trying to fulfil these functions. For years after the General Strike there were very few large-scale confrontations between employers and unions and so this side of the Council's work fell largely into disuse. More recently, however, national confrontations have again dominated the headlines and several times the Council has been called on to help union members. In 1971, for example, local Post Office workers benefitted from the active assistance of the Council during their stoppage. In 1972, a much more severe confrontation occurred when in July five London dockers were imprisoned for defying a judgement of the National Industrial Relations Court and it is interesting to note that it was a somewhat similar incident one hundred years ago which had called the Trades Council into existence. Within hours, in 1972, the Council had organised a protest meeting in Queen's Square, calling on the government to immediately release the dockers and on the labour movement for all possible support. That the Council acted so promptly on this occasion illustrates its continuing determination to uphold the independence of the trade union movement. Nevertheless, the fact that this meeting was not well attended shows that the Council had not entirely solved the problem of how to command the attention of those very trade union members it strives to represent. For since 1945 it has certainly been active in a range of valuable, if unspectacular ways. It has shown a keen interest in occupational health problems: it was, for instance, early in the field campaigning for cervical cancer screening facilities for women workers. It has sought to safeguard the rights of young workers under day release schemes and to see that union members are properly represented before the innumerable tribunals adjudicating cases arising out of welfare legislation. In these and many other ways the Council has striven to deserve the respect of the public and the support of trade unionists: it hopes to continue to do so in the future.

David Large and Rob Whitfield

Keeping the flame alight

1973—2023

"Kill the Bill" demanded the banners carried by supporters of Bristol Trades Union Council (BTC) in 1972. The Council had organised a train from Temple Meads to carry some 400 delegates and supporters to London to protest against the Heath government's Bill to restrict trade union rights.[98]. Two years later, that protest contributed to a partial victory—the election of a Labour government brought the repeal of Edward Heath's Bill. The election also put Ron Thomas, an active member of BTC, into Parliament as the MP for Bristol North West. He, like the majority of the Council, was strongly opposed to the Common Market and during his time as an MP he voted against the Labour government 137 times.

In the 1970s and 80s the Communist Party played an important role in the BTC, with Brian Underwood, Jack Evans, Ron Press and Bill Nicholas, all Party members, holding key positions on the Council's executive committee. In his memoir *Settling Accounts* Bill Nicholas is frank about the control he exercised: "When I was President of the Trades Council, they said 'Christ Bill! I think you were born on the steam roller'. I used to say, 'Shut up and sit down'."[99]

Mike Richardson, who was a delegate from his NATSOPA branch to the BTC in the late 1970s and early 1980s, described it as "bureaucratic and heavily controlled … Anything that seemed at all revolutionary, the Communist Party oddly enough would stamp their heels on it and say, 'this is not reality'."[100] He characterised the arguments on the BTC as the 'Trots' versus the 'Tankies'. The 'Trots' being left groups, like the Workers Revolutionary Party and the International Marxist Group, who were influenced by Trotsky's ideas, versus the 'Tankies', the Trotskyist label for Communist Party members on the basis that they had supported Russia sending tanks in to crush revolts in Hungary and Czechoslovakia. There was some embarrassment amongst Bristol Communist Party members when it emerged that a representative from Riga had been arrested after an exchange visit to Bristol because he had helped to organise a dock strike in Latvia[101], which was then part of the Soviet Union.

98 Bill Nicholas, *Settling Accounts*, Bristol Trades Council and South West TUC, 2008, p39.
99 Nicholas, p41.
100 Interview with Mike Richardson, 15 June 2022.
101 *Guardian*, 9 May 1978.

Dave Chapple, a veteran trade union activist, is sardonic about the BTC at this time, arguing that:

> it should have been dominated by the elected convenors and senior stewards of the largest city workplaces. Instead, it was dominated by self-styled Marxists of various kinds, most of whom did not actually represent that many workers … Communist Brian Underwood, always the main speaker from the BTC Executive, dominated most proceedings and stopped things getting too far to the left—in particular the wording of motions which would get ruled out of order.[102]

Mike Richardson recalled caucus meetings to resist Communist Party dominance, held immediately before BTC meetings, and these included some on the left of the Labour Party as well as the 'Trots.' For a brief period in the early 1970s, the BTC provided a platform for a publication called the *Bristol Socialist* which argued for workers control in the aircraft industry. But the Communist Party reasserted its control in 1974 and the BTC's support for the paper was withdrawn.

The issue of Northern Ireland came up frequently at BTC meetings but there was little consensus, even amongst the caucus, especially after an IRA bombing in Bristol in 1974. In the early 1970s the BTC opposed the Prevention of Terrorism Act which led to the expulsion of Danny Ryan, a BTC delegate, from the UK in 1975, but rejected motions calling for Ireland's re-unification and for removing British troops from Northern Ireland.[103]. Ann Hope from the Belfast Trades Union Council told the Bristol Trades Union Council on 20th November 1975 that "Troops Out Now would be a disaster."[104]

Nevertheless, the issue resurfaced at a meeting on 21st July 1977. "This BTC urges H.M.'s Government to make an immediate declaration of intent to withdraw militarily and politically from Northern Ireland and to initiate an immediate discussion with the Republic of Ireland to consider the security, political and economic needs and to help

---

102 Dave Chapple's memoir *Bristol, 13 miles due east*, Somerset Socialist Library, 2021, p51.

103 When I was working in Dublin in 1979, I met Danny Ryan to express sympathy with him about what I had seen as his unfair expulsion but he seemed keen to stress his closeness to Irish paramilitaries.

104 Trades Council minutes held in the Bateman section of the Special Collection of the University of Bristol library. These are quoted frequently in subsequent pages. Although there were occasions when Republican and Loyalists united over trade union issues, there were sharp sectarian differences in the Northern Ireland trade union movement at the time.

implement this withdrawal as quickly as possible." There was an amendment to delete all the words after Ireland but this was defeated by 39 votes to 21. The original motion was then carried with 42 in favour and 16 against.

The issue continued to be a contentious one and when a motion calling for affiliation to the International Tribunal on the British presence in Ireland came up in June 1978, it was rejected. In September 1984 a delegate wrote to complain that the BTC had failed to back a Troops Out demonstration. In 1986 the BTC learnt that Pete Jordan, a former delegate to BTC, had been sent to prison for 14 years for attempting to kill a Major Baty, who had served as an SAS officer in Northern Ireland.

Facing up to the fascists

Phillip Gannaway, the local chairman of the National Front (NF), occasionally turned up to the BTC as an EEPTU delegate but almost all members of the BTC were strongly opposed to the NF, an ultra-right-wing party led nationally by John Tyndall. However, there were differences about the best way to respond. A large and active branch of the Anti-Nazi League emerged in Bristol but, partly because it was initiated and driven by the Socialist Workers Party, it was seen by the Communist Party as 'Trotskyist' and officers of the Council were wary of involvement. "We had quite a bit of a problem supporting anything that was SWP," said Andy Robertson, a former President of the Council, "we tended to find that whatever decision was made, they'd do it their own way. So we were a bit pissed off with that"[105].

Although the BTC made a donation to the Bristol Anti-Nazi League, its rapid growth seems to have given it some organisational problems and, on 23rd September 1978, Ted Moore, the secretary of the Council, wrote to the local branch expressing concern, especially about the finances of Bristol ANL, and asking for a report. Mike Eaude, the ANL's local trade union officer who was also a member of the Council, apologised for a failure to respond previously and expressing the hope that the Bristol Trades Council remained committed to ANL. "We consider it extremely important to build a movement against racism and fascism, rooted in the trade unions."[106]

A later report from Mike Eaude and Ron Press, both Council members, acknowledged the weaknesses of Bristol ANL's organisational

105 Interview with Andy Robertson, 21 July 2022.
106 Bateman collection.

structures and finances. "Another weakness" it continued "not yet confronted, is that of relations with the black communities. The Bristol ANL is an almost totally white organisation."

The Council did make a donation to the Bristol ANL but its officers preferred to support its own initiatives—Bristol Campaign for Racial Harmony and the Bristol Festival Against Racism. Its march on 30th September 1978 was intended to be silent with only one slogan— "One Race, the Human Race" but this directive was ignored by ANL participants.

Grunwick gremlins

The Council was united in its response to the strike at Grunwick photo processing laboratories in 1976. The Grunwick management had rejected the claim of its mainly Asian workers for recognition of the union that they had joined (APEX—the Association of Professional, Executive, Clerical and Computer staff) and had sacked 137 of its workers as a result of the strike. Although it had little support initially, the response grew in significance and "encouraged white trade unionists and workers, for whom the strike was symbolic of workers' fundamental rights to be part of a trade union."[107]

On 16th June 1977, BTC passed a motion deploring "the violent intervention of the London police in the struggle of the workers at Grunwick for trade union recognition. We call upon the General Council" [presumably of the TUC] "to request all affiliated Unions to use their industrial power to bring to a complete halt the anti-trade union activities of Grunwick's management. We further call for the disbandment of the Special Patrol Group".[108]

A month later the BTC called for "mass picketing and boycotting of the factory" and on 15th August sent a delegation of members to the Grunwick picket, sponsoring a coach to transport the delegation. But by 20th October 1977 BTC support seemed to be flagging, with a motion for another mass picket on 7th November carried only narrowly, 28 in favour with 26 against.

Despite the eventual failure of the mass pickets to secure union recognition at Grunwick, this was a period when the BTC was at its

---

107 Robin Bunce and Samara Linton, *Race and the left* in *Rethinking Labour's Past*, I.B.Tauris 2022, p178.
108 A para-military unit of London's Metropolitan police service deployed against supporters of the Grunwick strikers in 1977 (and later responsible for the death of Blair Peach in 1979).

The plight of the mainly Asian women sacked from Grunwick Film Processing Laboratories stirred the sympathy of workers throughout the UK, including the BTC.

strongest, with unions throughout the UK flexing their muscles. "Unions grew steadily reaching their zenith in the 1970s and securing important wins such as equal pay for women."[109] The fact that there was a Labour government in power did not inhibit the BTC from expressing sharp criticism, especially on educational issues. On 21st April 1977 Sue Leque, a pupil at Hartcliffe School, told the BTC about the walkout and march by pupils at her school in protest at cuts in the local education budget made by Avon local government. The minutes recorded that "she received very warm and prolonged applause for her address."

A 21st September 1978 motion passed by the BTC articulated some of the reasons for the discontent in Bristol schools. It condemned "the attitude of the government in placing economic considerations over the wellbeing of school children and therefore resolves to support the action of the NUT in opposing the Government's proposals [for cuts in the education budget]".

The Council's strength in 1978 was demonstrated by a successful May Day march and rally addressed by Tony Benn. It had given support to refugees from the dictatorship of Pinochet in Chile and they were given a place in the rally. "Our comrades from Chile" reported Ted Moore, the Council's secretary, "entertained us for half an hour with

109 Eve Livingston, *Why We Need Unions*, Pluto Press, 2021, p13.

music and song from their own country. Although few could understand the words, our natural sympathy for people in exile, and the fight back in Chile, combined to give them a good reception and applause at the end of their performance."

He was less sure about the performance of the Left Turn Theatre Group who, he wrote, "put on an entertaining but terribly left-wing political sketch, which would not have pleased a certain County Council." That would have been Avon County Council with whom teachers were in dispute. On 22nd September 1978, the *Evening Post* reported the BTC's criticism of Avon Council under the headline "Schools Policy gets caning from Unions." There was also concern about attempts being made to restrict the 1967 Abortion Act and the BTC gave support to a national Trades Union Congress demonstration on the issue on 28th October 1978.

It was the beginning of what became known as 'the Winter of Discontent'. At its 14th December meeting the BTC gave its support to a local strike by the National Union of Journalists and "urges all citizens in Bristol to refrain from purchasing blackleg newspapers." There were widespread public sector strikes "in response to pay caps introduced by James Callaghan's Labour government in an attempt to control inflation. More than 29 million working days were lost to strike action and the inability of Callaghan's government to put an end to the strikes swept Margaret Thatcher's Conservatives to victory in 1979…"[110]

The BTC had attempted to encourage its members to work for a renewed mandate for Labour in the 1979 General Election but many trade unionists were disillusioned by the Labour government's priorities. According to Nathan Yeowell, the Winter of Discontent, as it was called, "shredded Labour's immediate claims to economic competence and heralded the popular exclusion of trade union involvement in national politics that was to characterize the decade to come." [111]

The shadow of Thatcherism

At the BTC's May Day rally in 1979, Tony Benn "touched upon policy decisions which he considered had eroded support and had led to a Tory victory." Soon after Thatcher's election, unemployment rose sharply and the BTC expressed its concern. Residents of St Paul's found a more direct way of expressing concern—a police raid on the Black and White

110 Eve Livingston, p14.
111 Nathan Yeowell, *Introduction to Rethinking Labour's Past*, p12.

Lloyds Bank burns during the St Paul's Rising of 2ⁿᵈ April 1980 that led to the BTC report *Slumbering Volcano?*

café in Grosvenor Road on 2ⁿᵈ April 1980 led to what became known as the St Paul's Rising. There were 13 arrests and 25 people, including police and press representatives, were taken to hospital.

On 17ᵗʰ April 1980, the BTC responded promptly, calling for a "full and open enquiry into the incidents in St Pauls" and Ron Thomas, who had lost his seat at the 1979 election, became its coordinator. It also, on 20ᵗʰ October 1980, passed a motion from the EEPTU which called for the establishment of an employment centre for the unemployed in the belief that the unemployed should be "taken under the control of the trade union movement."

The Thatcher government's ironically named Employment Act of 1980 outlawed secondary picketing and restricted the number of people who could be on the picket line. The 1982 Employment Act, writes Eve Livingston, "went even further, banning 'political strikes' and narrowing the grounds on which workers could take strike action."[112]

112 Eve Livingston, p14.

The first edition of the bulletin of the Unemployed Workers Centre
set up by the BTC.

In 1982 unemployment in the UK reached 3 million for the first time since the 1930s and by September 1984 the Unemployed Workers Centre at 27 Great George Street was up and running. Its *News No. 1* bulletin proclaimed that it was "back on the rails and working expressly for Avon's unemployed."

Meanwhile the enquiry initiated by BTC had produced the impressive *Slumbering Volcano?* report,[113] arguing in its first sentence that BTC represented "over 55,000 trade unionists" and going on to say that "At a well-attended meeting there was complete agreement that the 'authorities' had no intention of holding a full and open public enquiry." Its terms of reference were "to enquire into the social and economic conditions prevailing in the St Paul's area and to make recommendations which might ensure a level of communal harmony and stability sufficient to minimise the risk of a repetition of anything like the events of 2nd April 1980."

The report linked the BTC's concern to the lack of jobs, pointing out that "the scourge of unemployment falls more heavily on black workers, and especially on young black workers, than of whites of the same age … we have evidence that black youngsters with qualifications have to make many more applications than white applicants with equal or even lower qualifications in order to obtain an offer of employment."

After commenting on what it saw as "the disastrous effect" of the M32 dividing the St Pauls community, the report went on to criticise "the lack of a satisfactory community centre within the area." What is most striking about the report in retrospect is that some of its recommendations appear to have been listened to. There is now—at the Malcolm X Centre, opened in the early 1980s—"a new community centre at St Barnabas…run by a management committee which includes representatives of all ethnic groups" and the recommended library in the area is up and running. Furthermore the "strongly urged" solution for "the conversion of Fairfield and Cotham into neighbourhood comprehensive schools" has come to pass, though not until 2000/2001.

The report quoted from the 1980 Annual Report of the Bristol Council for Racial Equality—"Our experience in training police officers has revealed a considerable proportion exhibit strong prejudice" and advocated "specific training in community relations…for all police officers working in the area." That part of the report appeared not to

113 *Slumbering Volcano?* Bristol TUC, Bristol Archives 43129/Lib/StP/2/1/22.

have been responded to and the second St Pauls rising of 1986 was targeted at the police.

Delegate Betty Underwood also drew BTC's attention to "the sinister implications contained in the October 1993 Griffiths report on the NHS. It signified a move towards placing some health services under the control of private companies (outsourcing)."[114]

Printer's devil

For much of the 1980s BTC was preoccupied by disputes in the printing industry. Rob Whitfield had an insight into print trade unions shortly after he had co-authored the 1873–1973 history of the BTC. He had worked for Mardon, Son and Hall in Bristol and quickly become the Father of the Chapel there, in effect the SOGAT shop steward. He discovered that there were procedural agreements that "put union officials in a position where they could regulate union members and were highly valued by the employers." He eventually came to the conclusion that the full-time union officers he encountered were "remote, bureaucratic and controlling."[115]

In 1983 the National Graphical Association took on Eddie Shah, the owner of the Warrington Messenger, who, despite the closed-shop agreement, had sacked three NGA members for refusing to work with non-union members. On 12th December the BTC passed a motion giving "its full support to the NGA in its fight against the Tory government, the police and the employers who are involved in a conspiracy to destroy the basic democratic rights of the working class and its trade union movement…"

But the dispute, and those that followed it, opened up divisions over demarcation between the print trade unions. "Hereafter these difficulties" wrote Mike Richardson, a former member of BTC, "led to an increase in inter-union disputes, whose severity did not bode well for fighting any potential battle at News International." It was there that Rupert Murdoch had bypassed the print unions altogether by setting up an alternative printing set-up.

"Concerned about this development", recorded Mike Richardson, BTC wrote to the local branches of the NUJ, SOGAT and the NGA in August 1985, to establish a local standing committee for the printing and media industry." BTC stressed the importance of unity at a time

114 Mike Richardson, *Tremors of Discontent*, Bristol Radical History Group, 2021, p135.
115 Email from Rob Whitfield to author, 1 November 2022.

when a rogue union—the EEPTU—was reported as having signed an alleged no-strike agreement with Eddie Shah. "The SOGAT Bristol and West of England branch committee rejected this call and the initiative collapsed, compounding the long-held distrust prevailing, at all levels of both unions, between SOGAT and the NGA."[116]

There was more consensus in the BTC in opposition to restrictive abortion laws and in support for the Campaign for Nuclear Disarmament. On 20th October 1984 it was involved in an important Bristol conference on "Arms Conversion and the Economic Consequence of the Arms Race for Trade Unionists working in the defence industry."

Miners v Government

Squabbles between unions in the print industry were overshadowed by the miners' strike that began in March 1984 and a month later the BTC organised a meeting "in support of The Miners' Struggle". Despite some misgivings about the fact that the National Union of Mineworkers did not hold a ballot of its members on the strike, the importance of solidarity was obvious to delegates. BTC passed a motion on 13th September 1984 welcoming "the decision of the TUC at Brighton to mobilise the whole weight of the British trades union movement in support of the NUM in its critically important struggle in defence of jobs and the industrial bases of this country, a struggle which the NUM is fighting on behalf of all working people."

Fundraising events for the miners in Bristol included a supportive speech by actor Tony Robinson, immediately recognised by the Welsh miners who were at the meeting, as Baldrick—"I have a cunning plan"— from *Blackadder*. By 1985 it was becoming clear that the strategy of Arthur Scargill, the NUM's leader, was not cunning enough.

The defeat of the miners contributed to what Roger Thomas, current vice-president of the BTC, described as "a steep and precipitous decline[117]" of the Council, a decline apparent throughout the labour movement. There is a hint of concern about it in a BTC internal report in July 1986 which sought ways of "promoting better attendances." The Amalgamated Engineering Union, the Transport and General Workers Union and the General, Municipal, Boilermakers and Allied Trade Union had been the backbone of the BTC, said Roger Thomas, but all of

116 Mike Richardson, 'Leadership and Mobilization: SOGAT in the 1986–87 News International Dispute' in *Historical Studies in Industrial Relations No. 15*, Spring 2003, pp54–55.
117 Roger Thomas conversation with the author.

them emerged weaker from the Thatcher government's assault on trade unions. Between 1979 and 1998, the Tory government introduced seven anti-union laws. These included the outlawing of secondary picketing and political strikes, imposing onerous restrictions before strike action could be taken, removing union immunities, so allowing employers to bring injunctions, and legalising the sacking of strikers taking unofficial action.[118]

When Mike Richardson was sacked in 1986, he got wholehearted support from the BTC but that did not get him reinstated. By now there was a significant drop in numbers attending BTC meetings, just 15 or 20 delegates turning up sometimes. "A lot to do with Thatcherism, it was losing the clout that it did have at one time. A lot of left groups decided 'this is not worth our while; this is not going to change stuff'."[119]

On 7th May 1986 there was another rising in St Pauls, triggered by a raid of 600 police officers, nominally in response to drink and drug offences, though seen by some as revenge for the humiliation of the police in 1980. The BTC called for an independent enquiry. Three years later BTC meetings moved from Shepherds Hall to what became Tony Benn House.

In 1989 Bristol dockers came out on strike against the abandonment of the Dock Labour scheme. "We tried to get the BTC to criticise the Bristol City Council" recalled Mike Richardson "but they supported the South West TUC who just wanted to cave in."[120] The dispute reached a climax on 21st July 1989 at a BTC meeting attended by a large contingent of Bristol dockers. "In a highly charged atmosphere" wrote Mike Richardson later, "BTC, in a hotly disputed count, rejected the Bristol dockworkers request for the BTC to affiliate to the local Dockers' Support Group". When faced with an unofficial action that might be deemed political and unlawful, he saw the BTC's response as conservative and the outcome was the return of casual labour on the docks.[121]

BTC continued to organise marches on May Day and at one of them a group of anarchists attempted to take a leadership role. Don Bateman, then the BTC's President, spotted the anarchist black flag moving to the front of the march, grabbed the flag's carrier and wrestled him to the ground. By 1987 Don Bateman, who had contributed so much to BTC in different roles, was exasperated not only with attention-seeking

118 Kenan Malik, *Observer*, 9 October 2022.
119 Mike Richardson conversation with the author.
120 Mike Richardson conversation with the author.
121 Brh.org.uk/strike/articles/abolition-of-the-national-dock-labour-scheme

anarchists but also with the failure of the Trades Union Congress (TUC) to respond to correspondence and to take on a leadership role. "The TUC at times drives us mad with its incompetency...Why do we have to be embarrassed by our own inconstancies? Can you realise what the outside world thinks about us?"[122]

Disputes in the printing industry continued to be the main focus of the BTC. The print unions had been in dispute with the Arrowsmith company in Bristol in 1980 and in 1988. Then in 1993 the company sacked 122 workers and derecognised the union, despite the BTC giving the print unions their full support. Andy Robertson, who became BTC President, was one of those ousted from his job at this time, an industrial tribunal coming to the conclusion that this was because of his role as a shop steward. But he still didn't get his job back.

"Cumulatively, balloting legislation introduced government interference in the guise of regulation" writes Eve Livingston, "paring back union independence through the exercise of state power."[123] Although public support for the Tory government was slipping away, it was becoming clear that the unions could not expect much if a Labour government was elected. Tony Blair insisted, while still in opposition, that "the essential elements of the trade union legislation of the 1980s will remain."[124]

But the BTC did have a significant role involving trade unions in opposition to the Poll Tax. When it was first mooted in 1987, a motion passed by the BTC on 17th September saw that the outcome from it would be "that the wealthy will benefit and working people will be paying for more reduced local authority services." According to Roger Thomas it was able to coordinate opposition through the Anti-Poll Tax Federation. Some 5,000 people took part in a protest in Bristol on 6th March 1990. There was a mounted police charge followed by 26 arrests.

Things can only get better?

In May 1997 the BTC helped to secure at least one important victory after Labour won the General Election of that year. Fourteen members of the National Union of Civil and Public Servants had been sacked at GCHQ in 1984 because they refused to give up their trade union rights and the BTC stood by them in their long campaign. The newly elected

122 Letter from Don Bateman to Norman Willis, 14 July 1987.
123 Eve Livingston, p30.
124 Quoted by Kenan Malik.

The BTC had a significant role involving trade unions in the campaign against Thatcher's Poll Tax.

Labour government restored the union's negotiating rights and three of the sacked workers were able to resume their jobs with compensation—the others having either retired or moved on to other jobs.

But there was considerable concern over the new government's so-called 'Fairness at work' bill. The BTC's annual report for 1998–9 "condemned the Government's insistence that at least 40% of the entire bargaining unit must vote for recognition (40% Yes Vote Threshold) in a majority vote to create a 'Legal Right' to Trade Union Recognition for Collective Bargaining Purposes."

Karl Hansen is forthright about what happened under the Labour government. "Tony Blair's New Labour came to power after making a Faustian bargain that it would not upset Thatcher's settlement, leaving in place anti-trade union laws and paving the way for subsequent Conservative governments to further tighten the screws".[125] This seemed to demoralise many trade unions and attendance at the BTC shrank still further. Nevertheless, it was invited to participate in the Bristol Democracy Commission and went along with its 2001 recommendation for a directly elected Mayor for the city.[126]

Andrew Mathers was a member of the BTC for a time and could see its situation in a wider context. In an article that he co-wrote with

125 Karl Hansen, 'Criminalising Solidarity', article in *Tribune*, issue 15, 2022, p21.
126 *Local Democracy in Bristol*—final report of the Bristol Democracy Commission 2001.

Graham Taylor, he noted the drop in the number of Trades Union Councils in the UK, from 418 in 1982 to 138 in 2002. The writers commented on "very limited rejuvenation. Trades Union Councils on the whole are lacking in affiliation and delegate participation and are leaking officers who are largely white and increasingly elderly".[127] When there had been a proposal, on 18th January 1986, to form a black sub-committee this was firmly opposed by the BTC executive and the idea did not proceed.

So BTC remained overwhelmingly white—and overwhelmingly male too. When Sheila Caffrey, the current President of the BTC, turned up at her first meeting she was the only woman present and 'was asked "Excuse me, have you got the right room?"[128] Barbara Segal, from the UCU, had a similar experience "nobody took any notice of me".[129] But both came to see the BTC's potential which was expressed later in Andrew Mathers and Graham Taylor's article—"the role of political struggle in influencing the role and vibrancy of Trades Union Councils which have long been associated with forms of political radicalism that have resulted in persistent conflicts with the higher echelons of the TUC".[130]

And with the Labour government. Those conflicts were becoming apparent in the opposition to the invasion of Iraq in 2003 and in 2004 the RMT union and the FBU disaffiliated from the Labour Party. By now most of the full-time officials employed by trade unions no longer attended BTC, though Hugh Kirkbride (Unite), Rowena Hayward (GMB) and Andy Robertson (RMT) were exceptions. Andy Robertson highlighted the fact that trade union officials didn't like to criticise a Labour government too much but "the BTC is independent from the TUC, it's the rank-and-file speaking".[131]

Bristol blacklisting

Soon after the international financial crisis of 2008 UK unions found themselves up against the Conservative and Liberal Democrat coalition government. The Trade Union Act of 2016 "represented the biggest legal

127 Andrew Mathers and Graham Taylor, *Is there a future for community-based trade unionism in Britain?* Publishing Centre for Employment Studies, University of the West of England, November 2008. www2.uwe.ac.uk/faculties/BBS/BUS/Research/CESR/Nov2008MathersandTaylor.pdf
128 Interview with author.
129 Phone interview with author.
130 Mathers and Taylor, *Is there a future for community-based trade unionism in Britain?*
131 Conversation with the author.

In the campaign against blacklisting, BTC played a key role highlighting the involvement of Kier Ltd. Demonstration outside government offices in Bristol, 22nd June 2013.

International Workers' Memorial Day, 28th April 2023, commemorated by BTC.

attack on unions since Thatcher's reforms"[132] and BTC now had to fight on a number of different fronts.

As well as demanding a public enquiry into the second St Pauls rising, BTC got involved in the campaign against blacklisting of trade union activists, which had a particular Bristol focus. Workers on the Cabot Circus development were targeted and a key figure in the blacklisting was Cullum McAlpine who, write Dave Smith and Phil Chamberlain, "maintains impeccable social credentials with his membership of the Merchant Venturers—an exclusive club for Bristol businesspeople originally founded by slave traders".[133]

In 1989 the BTC had moved from meeting at Shepherds Hall to what was then called Transport House and discussions continued across the road at the Shakespeare or the Kings Head pub afterwards, often says Ian Wright, more interesting than the more formal debate that had preceded it[134]. The renovation work that was undertaken on Transport House meant that meetings had to move to St George Labour Club in 2011 temporarily and this negatively affected turnout. Trade unionists from Rolls Royce and Airbus who were once regular attenders at BTC no longer turned up, focussing their union activity instead on their workplace.[135]

"Meetings of the Trades Council were usually quite dry" according to Andrew Mathers, "with too much time spent listening to officers sitting at the 'top table' running through correspondence…Reports from delegates about their workplaces were few and far between yet when they did occur, such as about the situation on the docks at Avonmouth, the great potential of the Trades Council to connect trade unions from the roots up was manifest."[136] When Simon Crew became a delegate in 2000, he felt that he gained from learning of the experience of older members and after he became Vice President helped to initiate the erection of a Workers Memorial Plaque in Castle Park in 2006.[137]

In 2013, the BTC unanimously agreed to a motion from Bristol UCATT, the building workers' union, presented by their delegate Ian Wright calling for support "for a full investigation/public enquiry into blacklisting, both past and present and into the intimate involvement

132 Eve Livingston, p15.
133 Dave Smith and Phil Chamberlain, 'Blacklisted—the secret war between big business and union activists', *New Internationalist*, 2015, p161.
134 Interview with author 1 November 2022.
135 Phone conversation with Hugh Kirkbride, February 2022.
136 Email to author.
137 Interview with author.

of both the public and security services in these practices." The motion also aimed "to put pressure on Bristol City Council to refuse to accept tenders like Carillion and Kier" and this was followed up by getting the City Council to commit to refusing to award contracts to firms proven to be still involved in blacklisting. However, conveniently, this did not include those firms which had been involved in blacklisting in the past.

But Smith and Chamberlain point out in their *Blacklisted* book how difficult it was to organise effective resistance. Writing in 2013 they pointed out that "Government statistics indicate that only 18 percent of the workforce is now covered by any kind of collective agreement, with union density down to 15.5%."[138] In the same year the BTC meetings moved from the St George Labour Club back to what had become Tony Benn House.

In 2014 ACORN, the Association of Community Organisations for Reform Now, was established in Bristol. Its aim was to "organise communities rather than workplaces"[139] and Eve Livingston claims that in 2017 its campaigning stopped the city's mayor from scrapping council tax exemption for people on low incomes. "Bristol became the only major city to retain the full reduction, and £4m of public money stayed in the pockets of those who needed it most."[140] But BTC had not been involved in this campaign and had not linked up with a local community group in the way that had been suggested by Andrew Mathers and Graham Taylor in their 2008 article quoted earlier.

When the referendum on membership of the EU came up in 2016, BTC stuck to the anti-EU line it had taken in the previous referendum.

In 2017 the Taylor review on modern working practices reported but the government failed to implement most of its recommendations. Indeed, despite unions leading the fight for better conditions for insecure workers, notably at Uber and Deliveroo, the government has imposed an annual levy on trade unions that enabled strikers to be replaced by agency workers.[141]

Although the 2017 General Election result was better for Labour than had been anticipated, the outcome of the 2019 Election was a severe disappointment—"heartbroken about the result" was the way the BTC on-line record put it. "Trade unions" said the BTC website "will be a vital line of defence against the impact of the Tory government". But

138 Smith and Chamberlain, p99.
139 Eve Livingston, p92.
140 Eve Livingston, p83.
141 tuc.org.uk/sites/default/files/2022–07/InsecureWork.pdf

Labour mayor Marvin Rees didn't appear to think so—longstanding member Ian Wright points out that the BTC used have regular meetings with the City Council's Labour group and that the group used to take those meetings seriously and respectfully. But more recently the Labour group has not responded at all.

By 2019 the average attendance at BTC meetings, recorded in the BTC annual report for that year, was just eleven. Hugh Kirkbride, who served as the BTC President for a time, thinks that some unions, like Unite, moved their focus to the workplace, Rolls Royce and Airbus for example. But the BTC, he said, continued to support workers in struggle[142] and made a point of ensuring that Workers Memorial Day was commemorated. Like most voluntary organisations, BTC was hit hard by the Covid 19 pandemic but did continue to hold on-line meetings.

Barbara Segal believes that in recent years, especially since Sheila Caffrey from the National Education Union became President, the BTC has begun to come back to life.[143] Workers in dispute were invited to come and explain their issues at BTC meetings and the BTC aimed to have a presence at rallies in support of striking trade unionists. Recently too there have been more workplace branches represented relative to retired branches.

Ian Wright made a similar point, highlighting the times that the BTC has "taken a leadership role in organising rallies for workers in dispute—things are looking up."[144] An indication of the more optimistic attitude was apparent in the calling of a series of on-line key workers' summits linking Gloucester and District, Bath and Bristol's TUCs, during the period when they were not meeting in person. The downing of the Colston statue also helped to raise local morale and the 2020 annual report recorded that the BTC "has strongly supported the Black Lives Matter Movement and currently strongly supports the Colston 4 who are being so unjustly prosecuted." Eventually the jury found them not guilty.

BTC has also got involved in campaigns around Bristol's housing crisis, recently producing leaflets pointing out that BTC "is campaigning for secure and affordable housing for everyone." The leaflets make it clear that BTC is not confining itself to the traditional trade union role of improving wages and conditions. "We're pushing to stop rogue

142 Conversation with the author.
143 Conversation with the author.
144 Conversation with the author.

Bristol Trades Council marching at the Tolpuddle Festival, July 2014.

Supporting the RMT picket at Temple Meads station, June 2022.

landlords ripping-off desperate renters and for housing prices to be affordable, so people can choose what type of home they'd like for their family, as well as choosing where to settle."

Each year since the BTC placed a commemorative plaque in Castle Park, there has been a ceremony to mark Workers Memorial Day on 28th April. In 2021, recalls Simon Crew, it was especially poignant and relevant because of the accident at the Wessex Water site in Avonmouth the previous year. Four workers had been killed and relatives and friends brought bouquets of flowers in their memory.

In the same year there was the first meeting of the May Day Committee for many years, the "best attended meeting for several years" recorded the annual report and the 2022 May Day "the largest turn out for many years."[145] BTC also took part in the Bristol COP 26 protest. In a change from earlier policy, in December 2021, BTC unanimously agreed to support abolishing the position of Mayor of Bristol. Then in May 2022 the city arrived at the same conclusion, voting decisively to replace the mayor with a committee system.

More recently BTC has taken on a leadership role in organising rallies for workers in dispute. Striking workers have attended meetings to report on the progress of these disputes and this has led to an increased attendance at meetings.

Striking back

A TUC report in 2022 pointed out that "…as the living standards crisis has spiralled ministers have introduced more anti-union measures designed to hamper their ability to fight for their [rights]".[146] These measures have included imposing an annual levy of trade unions, introducing measures that will enable strikers to be replaced by agency workers and upping the damages employers can claim if unions inadvertently breach complex rules on industrial action. But that hasn't stopped them fighting.

Fifty years ago, it was the Communist Party that was the predominant influence in BTC but this is no longer the case. The Socialist Party (formerly Militant) now has some significant influence but BTC delegates have been able to work amicably during the recent revival of union militancy, regardless of specific political allegiances.

"Following the election defeat of 2019 and the shock of the

145 2021 Annual Report presented to 2022 AGM, 23 February 2022.
146 tuc.org.uk/sites/default/files/2022–07/InsecureWork.pdf

pandemic" wrote Amardeep Singh Dhillon in December 2002, "the trade union movement has effectively replaced the Labour left, creating its own campaigns and institutions and rhetorically and financially de-centering the Labour Party, in its own strategy".[147]

In the winter of 2022/3, the government threw down a gauntlet to trade unions in the U.K., not only resisting demands for wage increases to meet inflation but also proposing yet more anti-trade union legislation. The bill that would enable the government to demand 'minimum service levels' in the public and service sectors would in effect make industrial action illegal because it would be the business secretary who would define what that vague phrase means.

The BTC responded promptly and effectively to the government's challenge, deciding to host a march and mass meeting of the trade unions involved in industrial action on 1st February 2023—the National Education Union, the University and College Union, the Civil Service Union, the Rail and Maritime Union and the Association of Locomotive Engineers and Firemen. At a BTC meeting on 18th January 2023 to prepare for that meeting, Sheila Caffrey the President spoke of it being "a very exciting time in the workers movement, a time when we can make sure our voices are heard."

The massive turnout on 1st February inspired an exultant entry of the BTC's Facebook page: "What a show of strength and solidarity today! Over 6,000 marching through Bristol after at least 70 picket lines this morning! We can't be ignored when we stand together in such numbers!"

The Bristol Historical Association pamphlet on the BTC, written fifty years ago, concluded that "the Council has not entirely solved the problem of how to command the attention of those very trade union members it strives to represent." This continues to be true but its swift response to the 2022/3 crisis for the labour movement demonstrates that when delegates act in comradeship and solidarity, representing their workmates rather than any particular political faction, the BTC can still play an effective role in achieving a better society.

Colin Thomas

---

147 Amardeep Singh Dhillon, *A New Cycle of Struggle—the British Left Post-Corbyn*, December 2022
https://library.fes.de/pdf-files/bueros/london/19989.pdf

Book List

Further reading from Bristol Radical History Group:

Strikers, Hobblers, Conchies & Reds—Dave Backwith, Roger Ball, Steve Hunt, Mike Richardson

Bread or Batons?—Dave Backwith and Roger Ball

The Origins and an Account of Black Friday, 23rd December 1892—Roger Ball

Refusing to Kill—Jeremy Clarke, Lois Bibbings, Mary Dobbing, Colin Thomas

Ben Tillett—Jim McNeill

The Bristol Strike Wave of 1889-1890, Parts 1 and 2—Mike Richardson

Bristol and the Labour Unrest 1910-14—Mike Richardson

The Maltreated and the Malcontents, Working in the Great Western Cotton Factory 1838-1914—Mike Richardson

Men of Fire—Mike Richardson

Tremors of Discontent—Mike Richardson

Turbulence—Mike Richardson

The Enigma of Hugh Holmes Gore—Mike Richardson

Bristol Bus Boycott—Silu Pascoe (forthcoming)

Other relevant publications:

Settling Accounts—Bill Nicholas (Bristol Trades Council and South West TUC, 2008)

Why we need unions—Eve Livingston (Pluto Press, 2021)

Blacklisted—the secret war between big business and union activists—Dave Smith and Phil Chamberlain (New Internationalist, 2015)

Bristol 13 miles due east—Dave Chapple (Somerset Socialist Library, 2021)

Rethinking Labour's Past—edited by Robin Bunce and Samara Linton (I.B.Tauris, 2022)

Picture Credits

Pages iv, 24, 30, 44— Stills from *100 Years of Struggle* produced by the Bristol Trades Union Council, directed by Colin Thomas, transmitted by BBC Bristol in 1973.

Page 2—commons.wikimedia.org/wiki/file:london_trades_ demonstration.jpg.

Page 8—*Bristol Post* .

Page 9—Courtesy of Bristol Libraries.

Page 12—Courtesy of Bristol Archives.

Page 14—Scenes from the Military Invasion of Bristol, 23rd December 1892. The Diary of W H (Harry) Bow, 1892. Courtesy of Bristol Archives 31416/2.

Page 16—Courtesy of Bristol Archives.

Page 19—Taken from *The Apostle of Free Labour: The Life Story of William Collinson Founder and General Secretary of the National Free Labour Association* by William Collinson (Hurst and Blackett, 1913). Available on archive.org.

Page 20—Walter and Bertha Ayles, Souvenir of the opening of The Kingsley Hall, Old Market, 1911. Courtesy of Bristol Central Reference Library.

Page 28—Courtesy of the Working Class Movement Library.

Page 43—commons.wikimedia.org/wiki/File:Ernest_Bevin_MP.jpg.

Page 43—Courtesy of Dave Chapple.

Page 55—*The Morning Star*.

Page 57—*Bristol Post*, 2 April 1980.

Page 58—Courtesy of Special Collections, University of Bristol Library.

Page 64—Courtesy Dave Chapple.

Page 66—Blacklisting—Unite the Union.

Page 66—International Workers' Memorial Day—BRHG.

Page 70 (x2)—Courtesy of Roger Thomas and Barbara Segal.

Acknowledgments

Bristol Radical History Group is very grateful to the Bristol Historical Association for permission to reprint its earlier history of the Bristol Trades Union Council as part of this publication.

Many thanks to BTUC delegates who have given me helpful advice, especially those—like Ian Wright and Barbara Segal—who are also members of the Bristol Radical History Group. I am especially grateful to Rich Grove for his artwork and to Richard Musgrove who made sure that the publication was as accurate as possible and sustained my morale when, partly because of the shortage of minutes and annual reports covering the last thirty years, it sometimes felt that this publication would never be completed. If there are errors of fact or judgement, the responsibility is mine.

Colin Thomas